IDEA, FORM ARCHITECTURE

Design Principles in Contemporary Architecture

Egon Schirmbeck

Translated by Henry J. Cowan

VNR **VAN NOSTRAND REINHOLD COMPANY**
New York

D1448741

English language copyright (c) 1987 by Van Nostrand Reinhold Company Inc.

German language copyright (c) 1983 by Karl Kramer Verlag

Library of Congress Catalog Card Number   86-9050

ISBN 0-442-28219-2

Printed in the United States of America

Designed by Rosa Delia Vasquez

Van Nostrand Reinhold Company Inc.
115 Fifth Avenue
New York, New York 10003

Van Nostrand Reinhold Company Limited
Molly Millars Lane
Wokingham, Berkshire RG11 2PY, England

Van Nostrand Reinhold
480 La Trobe Street
Melbourne, Victoria 3000, Australia

Macmillan of Canada
Division of Canada Publishing Corporation
164 Commander Boulevard
Agincourt, Ontario M1S 3C7, Canada

16 15 14 13 12 11 10 9 8 7 6 5 4 3 2 1

Library of Congress Cataloging-in-Publication Data

Schirmbeck, Egon.
  Idea, form, and architecture.

  Translation of: Idee + Form + Architektur.
  Bibliography: p.
  Includes index.
   1. Architecture, Modern—20th century. 2. Archi- tectural design. I. Title.
  NA680.S3713 1986   724.9'1   86-9050
  ISBN 0-442-28219-2

Contents

Foreword

The author of this book on the relationship of idea to form and architecture is an architect who, in spite of his youth, has designed a number of excellent buildings. He is therefore not concerned with abstract theories but with the process by which an original concept influences the realization of an actual building. He appreciates the fact that the concept must be modified and altered in the course of the design process, because the problems confronting the architect become clear only during the design. Therefore, an idea encompasses not merely an original concept but also the modification and alteration that it undergoes during the design process.

This investigation, like every other concerned with the manifold phenomena of contemporary architecture, has had to be limited in scope. However, it covers a broad spectrum of present-day architecture, even though many other architects could have been included in the discussion.

To analyze the nature of the buildings, the author employs not merely text but also the analytical drawings that are so familiar to architects. Although these are in themselves abstractions, they have the advantage of immediate accessibility. The author notes at the end of his book that they do not resolve the question of how the user, for whom the architecture is intended, perceives and experiences the goals expressed by the architect in the form and shape of the building. This could only be answered by empirical investigations of contemporary buildings after a long period of occupancy.

The real value of this book, both for the architect and the student of architecture, lies in its method, the examination of the effect of ideas on action, and of action on ideas. If people complain about the irrelevance of contemporary architecture in meeting the needs of the user, this is because architects have spent too much time on abstract design and too little on reflecting on what has been accomplished.

JÜRGEN JOEDICKE

Introduction

The design activity of the architect consists of a multitude of individual decisions and evolutionary phases. In the end a planning concept evolves that is the model for future realization. Step by step, this planning concept is transformed into the final design through drawings, taking into account a number of individual problems, such as the requirements of form, function, technology, biology, ecology, and local government regulations.

In every design it is the task of the architect to reconcile the sometimes conflicting objectives of a new building and to propose a solution within the available means of construction. Every solution, and every building, mirrors in its entirety all the essential goals, requirements, or ideas in constructional form.

Apart from meeting the requirements, which should previously have been clearly defined and quantified as data, the suc-

cess or failure of the solution depends essentially on the adequate application of appropriate architectural principles. In recent years architects have been confronted with numerous demands resulting from theoretical planning discussions and from attempts at user participation in the planning process. In the process it became clear that the resulting goals and principles could not readily be transformed into action for a realistic design. On the contrary, during the last few decades a series of formal elements has been assumed uncritically from the Modern Movement, without considering the original goals; this created the potential for misunderstanding.

In the analysis of the design principles, an attempt has been made to describe and relate them to the constructional means available for the realization of the design. To illustrate the design activity of the architect, individ-

ual characteristics are illustrated by abstract sketches, analogous to the synthesis of design. These analyses attempt to relate retrospectively the various design decisions to the corresponding design elements. At the same time, a number of individual buildings are described to illustrate movements and trends in contemporary architecture and their dependence on formulated design maxims.

In chapter 1 the theme of "design" is discussed, and its goals and resulting operations determined and outlined. The derivation of the analysis from the design principles is also described.

In chapter 2 diverse buildings and projects from the 1960s and 1970s are analyzed. The individual design principles are enumerated and illustrated by sketches of building forms.

In chapter 3 description, comparison, and contrast of the principles are followed by a classification and graphic presentation of their significance in distinctive periods of the development of modern architecture. The main purpose of the analyses is to attempt a description of the diverse design ideas and the resulting architectural characteristics in the form of sketches of the design elements. In the process, the relationship between design principles and the realized built forms is made evident.

The analyses show that the overall form of a building is determined by relatively few design principles. The number of fundamental and characteristic principles that determines the overall concept of three-dimensional design is limited and can easily be kept in view by the designer. These principles can be used as guiding concepts at various levels of planning. The much larger number of specific design decisions are developed subsequently without explicit formulation of goals.

By limiting the analysis to typical characteristics of individual architectural movements, it can be shown that all goals and/or formulations of principles are essentially qualitative. Quantitative aspects of the development of new architectural forms are barely detectable. Corresponding to the categories of building characteristics in individual design concepts, one can recognize three essential types of principles as significant for the design of buildings. For example, one can determine the form of a building or the allocation of space primarily by rational considerations, such as structural principles, building services, or specific user requirements. These types of principles may be called "rational principles."

A second category of principles deals with built form and consequently the influence on the observer of the symbolic content of architectural elements. This aspect has acquired particular importance during the recent past in discussions on architecture.

Although the implementation of "rational" and "symbolic" principles may have specific and different psychological consequences, there are also principles whose expressed purpose is to produce specific psychic responses in people. These "psychological principles," for example, may aim at solutions that ensure user participation in the planning and design process or the feasibility of social contacts through appropriate layout of architectural spaces.

The limits of the individual types of principles are fluid, or at least there is a certain amount of cross-fertilization. The analysis of individual designs shows that in the period 1945–60, rational considerations have most influenced architecture; only in the very recent past have symbolic and psychological aspects again received special attention. The analysis also shows that formulated principles are not of equal importance at all levels of planning.

The establishment of relationships between formal principles and the architectural characteristics of individual architectural spaces has been attempted throughout this book. The individual design elements are shown in each case in graphic form. By describing the original background of the architectural form, this analysis should help at the same time to reduce the possibility of an incorrect interpretation.

A special attempt has been made to draw attention to the various movements and trends in contemporary architecture for each of the design elements, with special reference to the creativity of the architect.

Design in the Planning of Buildings

The Theme

The terms "design system," "structural grid," "architectural theory," "design theory," and "design concept" all denote aspects in the planning stage of design. Even though they are distinctively different concepts, they all define a certain task in the building process by means of individual, basic principles or goals. This multitude of concepts demonstrates that architecture differs from other scientific disciplines. In accordance with strict scientific principles, the concept of a system denotes a "multitude of elements and a multitude of relations which exist between these elements" (1). A one-sided procedure of this type for the ordering of spatial elements and their interrelationships in the design process is only possible under certain conditions. The structures (which are the task of the architect) are developed three-dimensionally from building elements, using generally formulated ideas, goals, theories, or programs. To this extent, a consensus is possible with regard to widely differing design systems or principles of order.

The concepts of "design theory" or "architectural theory" are often given varying interpretations. Christian Norberg-Schultz is of the opinion that the word "theory" is so threadbare and often so far removed from practical considerations that hardly anybody still believes architectural theories produced by architects once had direct significance for the practice of building (2). However, the value of theories, at least in the past, can in fact be determined unequivocally by the numerous testimonials to the quality of the architecture of great theoreticians and architects such as Vitruvius, Alberti, Palladio, Schinkel, and Le Corbusier. During their periods of influence, their theories had an authority far greater than any theories do today.

Today, architectural decisions can be made on the basis of valid theories that are used in professional practice. However, these derive essentially from the realm of economics, industry, or administration. Decisions on the quality of architecture are made primarily on the basis of economics, finance, organizational and production technology, and their value systems. One can hardly claim equal acceptance in this decision-making process for any theory of architecture that defines the principles of design in the form of a man-ecology system. There is merely a multitude of individual theories or ideologies. Architects develop theories in accordance with their personal conception of the material and immaterial values within architecture, on the basis of life experience; indeed, all architects must formulate their own goals or principles (as theoretical concepts or ideas) in order to use them as arguments or criteria for implementation in appropriate buildings. This fact has been responsible in recent years for the paucity of any meaningful application in architectural practice of discussions based on scientific or architectural theories. As a statement, this is not news. Even if one confines oneself to the supplementation of the above-mentioned theories from other disciplines with so-called explicit criteria and quantitative characteristics, it is still necessary to develop architectural theories, which are accepted as being of equal value, in order to achieve the desired goals in each case.

In statistics about the activities of architects, one hears time and again that design accounts for only about 5 percent of the total work load (3). With this statement one attempts at the same time to place a value on the design process and to limit the time available for it. It is true that a number of architectural tasks require far more time than design does. However, this obscures the significance and consequences of the individual decision-making phases in the work process. In the hierarchy of planning problems, it can be shown (4) that within this "5 percent activity," decisions must be made that are of fundamental importance for the function or form of the building. Fundamental decisions are also made in this phase that determine the overall concept of the architectural solution; and goals are set that will continuously influence all the details of function, construction, and form. So it is evident that all the essential steps in planning derive directly or indirectly from the decisions and goals fixed at the design stage. The needs of the individual users and the demands they make on the design of the building are determined and defined at this initial stage of decision making.

It should be emphasized that none of the individual activities has a primary and specific claim on the architect's time. For example, comprehensive design concepts can achieve their goal (or benefit the user) only if the designer has the scope to develop a constructional scheme and realize it within an "optimal" technical and commercial framework. To avoid misunderstanding, it should be mentioned immediately that there is no logical sequence of steps in design. Revisions of the goals made in the beginning ultimately determine the design process. Venturi even considers it legitimate to define the ultimate goal of a design only after one has backtracked to it during a modification (5).

The reasoned description of the actual intention or goal, related to the architectural means employed, is of importance in addition to the actual design process, because the desired function, construction, and shape can be achieved only if the architect has adequate architectonic means, or design elements, to put these goals or ideas into practice. So far, attention has scarcely been drawn to the dependence of the achievement of the goals of architectural planning on the availability of the architectonic means available for their realization. The presentation of the interdependence of goals and means may be of some help in clarifying the activity of design in this discussion. Furthermore, it assists a detailed understanding of the movements and trends in the development of architecture, and it may indicate appropriate future action for the design activity of the architect.

The Contemporary Situation

The development of a design concept is determined by a series of influence factors (design principles). In previous centuries of the history of architecture, the characteristics of quality—that is, the "theories" of architecture—were firmly set down, and their influence on form was unequivocally stated in terms of precise directions (by Vitruvius, Alberti, Palladio, Schinkel, Le Corbusier, and Mies van der Rohe, among others). Some of the last comprehensive concepts for creative architecture were set out at the beginning of the twentieth century by groups such as the De Stijl movement, by representatives of the functional building concept such as Hugo Häring or Hans Scharoun, and by individuals such as Gaudí or Le Corbusier. Their work was largely based on comprehensive architectural theories, whose goals, consequences, and interpretations are even today the subject of controversy and discussion.

A discussion of the principles of architecture and of design started again, after a pause, during the last few years. Thus, Charles Jencks (6) speaks of a "method of design" to develop a "double-coded" architecture. Many of the contributors to the present debate refer to general considerations in the history of architecture, of art, or of culture.

These ideas depend on a multitude of factors influencing a certain period of time. They are determined by social, cultural, political, or climatic conditions. Theories about architecture and its relevance have existed, starting with Vitruvius, for more than two thousand years. Form and technology were time and again interpreted as the creative content and the symbol of the function of the building. In that process, form was frequently iso-lated as the expression of fine art, as opposed to technology and science. For example, Philip Johnson, the friend and pupil of Mies van der Rohe, answered the question whether one should consult a sociologist, with: "For heaven's sake, no!—They do not know how to build a city; only artists know that!" (7). Statements of this kind today serve at best to boost an individual's ego, or they smack of utopianism. At the same time, they describe very clearly the dilemma of the architect's field of activity; that is, it is almost impossible to give people in other specialized disciplines, who are concerned with planning, any direct description of the architect's procedure when he is engaged in design. Heinrich Klotz (8) mentions the same problem in a talk with Hans Kammerer, in which he discusses the contribution of Alexander Mitscherlich to a planning commission, and the relevant descriptions of the architectural procedures. While other specialized disciplines can present and analyze a number of problems for architects, it is left entirely to their imagination and innovation how they interpret these problems and the contradictions inherent in them, and especially by what architectural means they propose to solve them. There are no direct rules as to how architects should act in those circumstances.

According to Gerhart Laage, the newer architectural theories no longer concern themselves with "only art, only technology, or only products," but at least in part with a more comprehensive "man-environment relationship." Their essential concern for the planning and realization of architecture is first to make decisions on the desired social, commercial, and technical goals and then to find adequate means for design and construction (9).

In the public discussions of the last few years, the architect has not really succeeded in offering society solutions for an environment that provides the user with a high workplace standard or high-quality habitation. Examples of contemporary architecture are designated by catchphrases like "monotony" or "inhuman architecture," and the architect is held responsible for all the negative consequences of this development. In the 1960s there was a parallel development in the literature on the work of the architect—its fundamental principles, the range of work, and the methods for doing this work and the associated planning. Architectural design was to be redeveloped systematically and "optimized" through functionally and technically perfect procedures, which are repeatable. Sociology, psychology, and other specialized disciplines were to contribute to giving architecture a "human" face. Catchphrases such as "user participation" and "appropriate scale," and demands for better communication between the user and the architect, made the architect feel insecure, a technician in opposition to the needs of society.

One of the problems lay in the difficulties of communication between different disciplines. Another problem lay surely in the fact that the architect, at the decisive stage of planning and design, was left "on his own"; that is, no one was able to suggest concrete action to the architect when he came to the real planning problems (10).

In the meantime, past experience may offer the architect some guidance on how to avoid a repetition of past failures (11). It is essential that the technical requirements of construction are met; in addition, proper consideration must be given to the user's goals, the demands of an architectural form, and the specific requirements of a particular building project. Furthermore, there may be a major misunderstanding with the client, unless the architect formulates and presents his own goals in unequivocal form.

Goals

In describing and analyzing actual examples of contemporary archi-

tecture, one can discern different, even contradictory goals. At a second stage of the analysis, one can contrast the building elements or built forms that have been used by individual architects to achieve these particular goals. It is then possible to determine which of the goals and ideas determine the development of contemporary architecture; which of the problems are potentially solvable by the architect; and what architectural means are at the disposal of the architect to enable him to translate his ideas into reality.

It is initially of no consequence whether it is possible to describe exactly the interpretation of the goals at any given moment. What matters is the relationship of an idea and of an architectural form to a given problem.

An attempt has been made to produce design principles to describe the interdependence of goals and of their realization in built form: design principles, such as are described by the HOAI (Honorarordnung für Architekten und Ingenieure) (12), that define the activity of the architect. Paragraph 15, Sections 2 and 3, defines the basic function of initial planning thus:

• Analysis of the principles;
• Determination of goals (boundary conditions, conflicts between goals);

• Drawing up a catalog of goals related to planning (programming goals);
• Design planning (planning of systems and their integration) as basic performance: "Detailed work on the planning concept (step-by-step elaboration of the drawings) considering the requirements of town planning, form, function, technology, environmental physics, energy, commerce, biology and ecology."

The essential performance of the architect is defined unequivocally in this statement. It is the architect's task to combine the different goals and demands that the building must meet and to propose a solution by architectural means. Each solution to a building problem, that is, each building, therefore mirrors in its entirety the essential goals, demands, and ideas in built form.

It is an essential goal of this analysis to describe examples of goal-setting for future planning and their translation into built reality in accordance with defined systems of design and order. Backtracking analyses of this kind can rarely be found. The interpretation of a particular type of architecture is based on this "catalog of planning-related goals" (HOAI) and the information regarding the "stepwise elaboration of the drawings" (HOAI). The examples so produced may serve as a basis and as a stimulus for the derivation of new planning concepts.

An attempt will be made to select a range of examples within the field of modern architecture to illustrate the diversity of contemporary architecture and its principal movements and trends. The beginning of the 1970s was a turning point in contemporary architecture, marked by the following events and developments:

1. Theoretical discussions of architecture were resumed at the beginning of the 1970s with contributions by Robert Venturi in *Complexity and Contradiction in Architecture* (13) and by Venturi and Denise Scott Brown in *Learning from Las Vegas* (14). A basis for an apparently new architectural symbolism was discovered in the process, with architecture becoming the carrier of expression and images with communicable content (15). The authors are of the opinion that architectural form and significance should not merely be appreciated by the abstract artistic concepts of ''quality'' and ''originality'' but also with the aid of popular pictures and signs that everybody understands, even though they may, in aesthetic terms, be borrowed or copied from elsewhere; the Las Vegas Strip is specifically quoted as an example. It is not only the functionalists who consider themselves under attack by Venturi's pleading for a symbolic architecture.

2. According to Klotz (16), the second hallmark of a decisive turning point was the discovery during the last few years that ''we must consider every single new building to a much greater extent in relation to its surroundings: architecture is ecology! The overconfidence of modern architecture had until then to a great extent ignored its impact on its surroundings. The movement for the preservation of monuments can claim a large share in this change of attitude.'' The concept of ''adaptive or integrated buildings,'' called by James Stirling ''repair of the city,'' has posed a question for all functional architecture.

3. Charles Jencks, in *The Language of Post-Modern Architecture,* critically reviews the development of modern architecture. He pithily analyzes the death of modern architecture and makes a case for an eclectic development of ''Postmodern'' architecture. Jencks defends the present move in the direction of confusion and eclecticism and concludes that an architecture will develop that will resemble the style of eighty years ago, which produced Neo-Queen-Anne and Neo-Edwardian styles in England. For him, this ''radical'' eclecticism is multivalent, in contrast to modern architecture (17). Such a decisive condemnation of modern architecture and an open leaning toward a symbolic ''pluralism of styles'' was hitherto unknown.

4. Besides the change in the ''internal'' content of modern architecture, the beginning of the 1970s was also remarkable for an ''external'' event, which may equally be considered a turning point: the ideas and concepts of a new architecture and of utopias for new buildings were once again presented in exquisitely drawn architectural sketches. Whole cities were perfectly presented in these graphic works of art. The charm of these architectural presentations, by themselves, offered hope for a change for the better in the environment through architecture. Plans, layout plans, details, and isometrics by Peter Cook were exhibited in a London gallery and offered for sale. The work of several groups persuaded us, through sensible graphic presentation, to accept a narrow architectural vision—for example, the ideas of the Rationalists or of Leo and Rob Krier. The artistically significant architectural drawing was moved back to the center of architectural discourse.

The analytical part of this book limits itself to the discussion of design principles and architectural realizations, using examples from contemporary architecture that are characteristic of the 1970s. The effect of the present-day debate on architecture may be evaluated by historians in the year 2000. The result of these explanations can presumably be used only by the next generation of architects. This means that conclusions on the goals and ideas of the present-day striving of architects can only be drawn at a much later point in time. However, architects today need to derive goals and solutions for tomorrow's architecture from the present situation. That is the reason for this analysis of examples drawn from present-day architecture.

The Steps in the Analysis

1. Statements on design in the planning of buildings/Theories in architecture/Concepts and definitions.

2. Analysis of examples of contemporary architecture selected according to their design goals or design ideas, and comparison with their solutions in the built form.

3. Comparison of goals, which are the present aim of architecture. Characteristics of the architectural means (elements of design that are at the disposal of the architect for a solution to the problem).

Limitations

The reason for the restriction of this analysis to selected examples drawn from contemporary architecture has already been explained. A further limitation lies in the choice of a few significant representatives of contemporary architecture. This choice is subjective, and it will be explained within the framework of this book through the examples. An attempt will be made to demonstrate the different and often contradictory concepts of contemporary architecture through the analysis of individual characteristic theories and buildings. This analysis is an attempt to examine more closely a series of frequently cited, publicized, and discussed ideas and concepts with particular reference to the design activity of the individual architects and their implementation into architecture. While some of these ideas will dominate building in the 1980s and 1990s, other concepts will prove to be unrealistic and will be forgotten. At the center of this controversy is the attempt to describe the dependence of projected goals, often formulated verbally or in abstract terms, on the practicability of realizing them by the available means of architecture; that is, in terms of constructional elements. One might quote as an example extreme concepts that may provisionally be placed into one or the other group. It is essential to maintain an overview of currently discussed approaches, whereby new ideas are interpreted by new architectural methods. Specifically, design concepts by the following architects are presented, together with their expression in built form:

- Piet Blom
- Herman Hertzberger
- Hans Hollein
- Arata Isozaki
- Louis Kahn
- Charles Moore
- Aldo Rossi
- Oswald M. Ungers
- Robert Venturi

Principles of Design

The analysis of the design principles is intended to reveal the theoretical goals on which a particular collection of architectural concepts or an individual building are based. Some goals may be determined from pronouncements and responses. Insofar as architects have explained the reasons for their actual goals, or one can derive them from their context, they have been described directly with the goals themselves. The analysis of the design principles and the presentation of their relationship to the built form (architectural characteristics) should help to clarify the background of the design process in each case and to describe individual, actual design concepts of contemporary architecture in more detail. The abstract and schematic drawings are intended to demonstrate the individual architectural characteristics through corresponding (sketched) design steps. At the same time, one can show the actual architectural elements by which the architect realizes, or at least attempts to realize, each particular goal. It is one of the peculiarities of the design process and of architectural creativity that one cannot establish a direct causal relationship between every one of its phases and every architectural expression.

An appreciation of the essential goals, and the architectural means used to implement them in the design, is essential to an understanding of the individual architectural examples. This analysis is an attempt to reduce the written description in the literature, dealing with the discussion of architectural theories, to actual design and planning goals in order to describe more clearly the characteristic design intentions and the architectonic means currently used to implement them.

The presentation of the design principles and the architectural characteristics can essentially be divided into three parts:

1. A description of the use of architectural theory in the work of each individual architect. His general theoretical approach, his background, and his exposure to individual movements and trends are briefly presented.

2. A search for design principles, obtained from the literature, from conversations, from a description of the buildings, and from idea sketches. Analysis of the architectural characteristics of individual buildings, which have a direct relevance to the specifically defined principles of the individual architect. This part of the analysis is essentially limited to abstract sketches to illustrate the individual design elements clearly. An attempt has been made to backtrack on the original design process and dissect it into individual "design sketches" to show visually the interrelationship between the principles and the architectural methods for their implementation. The individual aspects of the corresponding planning level are shown in parallel to the design process to identify the design phase in which each principle is realized.

3. A summary and comparison of the individual design goals in sequential form and a presentation of the different architectural characteristics are intended to identify the principles that may be realized by a particular architectural method and to show which of these methods are available to the designer to achieve a particular goal. For an understanding of the design solution, it is always necessary to couple each planning goal with the appropriate architectural solution. The multitude of approaches prevalent today should contribute to the definition of a spectrum of possible approaches to a solution (and of the architectural methods available for the purpose).

Analysis of the Design Principles

Development of the Analyses

The analyses of the following designs and plans aim to present design and planning principles and the methods of their realization by architectural means. In the process, the individual design elements on which the particular designs are based are demonstrated through a pictorial presentation of their architectural characteristics. This analysis is developed alongside an account of the designer's activity to make the clearest and most unequivocal statement on behalf of the given architect. The result of the design is thereby regressively dissected into individual design components, related to defined design principles. The process of design (as a synthesis) is followed backwards and presented approximately in its individual phases of design and decision. Alongside this stepwise derivation of the built solution to the problem through design sketches and drawings, an attempt is made to present the corresponding design elements (that is, the architectural characteristics) both through text and through drawings.

Fritz Schumacher (1) defined three phases in the creation of a building:

1. the initial phase (the process of design or planning);
2. the middle (architectural characteristics and methods of building);
3. the goals (principles).

The aspects of the *initial phase*—that is, the process of design and planning—entered into the professional practice of the architect only about forty years after Schumacher had called for it. He had already nominated for the *middle phase* a series of design elements: "Formal methods, for example the interpenetration of bodies, horizontality, verticality, contrapuntal composition, the juxtaposition of different motives, as well as the interconnection of bodies and building elements." Furthermore, he mentioned building forms that are "determined by statics and construction, for example shell surfaces and structural skeletons, as well as color, paintings and sculpture" (2).

As far as possible, the individual architectural characteristics have been presented in abstract form; that is, without additional architectural features that have no primary influence on the particular goal under consideration.

The *goals* of the individual architects were expressed in the form of principles in "colloquial" or in "general" form (3). An

9

analysis of comments on design has shown that a further classification into "ideal" and "concrete" goals is not really possible, nor are there any criteria for "measurable magnitude" (4). The decomposition of goals (principles) into "partial" goals, or their representation in the form of a "tree of goals," was not considered relevant in view of the type of information on the individual designs.

Consequently, the general principles on which the particular design is based are given in the first column. These general principles are documented with literal quotations (denoted by quotation marks) or by paraphrased statements (denoted by crosses). To provide an appreciation of the meaning and the purpose of a particular formulation, the next column contains its justification.

The analysis has shown that the overwhelming majority of formulated principles has been followed immediately by a justification of these planning measures. Usually, the reason for the design concept and its realization becomes clear only through this explanatory addendum.

Following the discussion of the design process of the architect, it seemed sensible to present some of the architectural characteristics at the particular level of design. As a starting point, it has been assumed that under normal conditions a design develops by steps, from a treatment of the town planning aspects, via the problems of organizing the masses of the building, to the organization of the individual spaces. Backtracking to allow for factors that affect the use or function at any of the individual levels of design may require modifications to the design concept that has been developed by the previous steps. In contrast to the abovementioned lack of a hierarchy of goals, the sequence of architectural characteristics produced a logical chain of interactions at several levels of design. One can follow, for example, through several different design levels the demand for a "human architecture."

In particular, architectural characteristics were examined at the following design levels:

- Town-planning level
- Object level
- Zone level

The *town-planning level* comprises everything within the context of town planning, such as the existing buildings, the environment, the landscape, the topography, the infrastructure, and other aspects, insofar as they can influence a concept at that level. The *object level* comprises the actual relation of the buildings to other buildings in their immediate vicinity. The *zone level*, as the lowest step, concerns itself with the allocation of space and user zones and with construction details.

To avoid any misunderstanding, it should be pointed out that the transition between the individual design levels is fluid. Consequently, the relationships between the individual architectural characteristics should not be regarded as fixed. The determining factor is the sequence of the relationships. This is, for example, defined when formulating the town planning maxims and is then followed through as far as the choice of material in the statement made at the zone level. A further subdivision into additional design levels may be omitted in view of the statements that may be expected in relation to the principles and the architectural characteristics.

Since the designer expresses himself through sketches and drawings, the architectural characteristics are presented in the form of schematic sketches. This representation corresponds to the actual design activity and yields the actual design or the proposed concept of the solution as the sum of a number of individual sketches. The individual architectural characteristics are presented in written form next to the graphic presentation for the sake of clarity. These descriptions are likewise derived, at least partially, from the descriptions that the individual architects gave of their designs. The juxtaposition of the written description of the architectural characteristics with the two-dimensional graphic statement of an architectonic situation (which is in reality spatial), is of central significance to the activity of design. The superimposition and addition of a series of graphic solutions generates the actual design; that is, the modeling of spatial groupings that give precise details of the dimensions, the proportions, the principles of construction, and the materials to be used. Sketches, scale drawings, and supplementary descriptions are the means whereby a model of a reality planned for the future is presented—the three-dimensional space that forms the building.

The design of every building is the result of a multitude of functional demands and requirements and of objectives to create a particular shape; it is also the product of a series of countless decisions arrived at with the aid of various specialized disciplines. The development, and consequently the architectural expression of the design of a building, is influenced by economic, functional, technical, sociological, and other disciplines. Depending on the utilization of the building (for example, in industrial buildings), a few aspects may dominate. In other building types, such as single-family houses, other requirements may be irrelevant.

A number of general or self-evident goals for the planning of buildings, such as cost, provision of the necessary spaces and utilities, organization of function and form, alternative structural principles, and various other matters have not been considered in the analysis of the designs. These and similar requirements form the basis of every design; that is, they are aspects of specific functions. The information is not relevant as long as such self-evident goals have no significant influence on the design concept. An attempt has been made in the analysis to outline characteristic and central design principles as well as their realization within the significant movements and trends of contemporary architecture. The demands of the architecture of the future form an important part of this discussion.

Piet Blom

Piet Blom belongs to the younger generation of Dutch architects, who attempt through their buildings to respond to the inhospitable nature of our cities and the lack of form in their architecture (12, p. 5). This new movement in architecture, called Structuralism, started as a reaction to the functional concept of the Garden City. Its proponents began to recollect that individual people had individual requirements. A group of young architects influenced by Aldo van Eyck analyzed in detail the life-styles and the traditional buildings of old and so-called primitive peoples. Studies were made of the communities of the Pueblo Indians in New Mexico, the Dogon villages in West Africa, the rebuilt Palace of Diocletian in Split, and the inhabited Arenas of Arles and Lucca; these were intended to help rediscover

the original requirements of social life. The group formulated traditional forms of social life that contrasted with the then generally accepted life-style based on the "functional" city. It selected verbal images such as "casbah organisée" and "labyrinthian clarity," which appear to be paradoxes. The "organized casbah" reminds one of both the inner-city district in North Africa and of systematic order. Aldo van Eyck saw therein a solution, in which the twin phenomena "order and chaos" (12, p. 9) again play a special role for people living together.

A series of design concepts and buildings were realized as a consequence of this analysis of familiar life-styles. The essential goals of these projects were reforms in the patterns of living. The new and different requirements for the

architectural forms of the future produced new or almost unknown groupings of rooms and buildings.

A further goal of the Dutch movement of architectural thought was the production of "structures" or "forms" over a period of time, which would remain entities from their beginnings through their further growth and would not lose the coherence of their parts.

A further important consideration in the discussion of new or traditional life-styles lay in a preoccupation with the transitional region of communication that provides contact between people. Leaving some of the rooms for the user to decorate is an important ultimate goal of this discussion. These principles conflict with those of the generally known "functional" city. The concept of the "organized casbah'' of Aldo van Eyck signifies the twin phenomena of this architectural concept of "order and chaos.'' According to this concept, rooms are to be created that take account of the human spirit, and at the same time give a better chance for the development of split twin phenomena, such as "individual/society,'' "part/unity,'' "interior/exterior,'' "much/little,'' or "movement/repose.''

The most obvious external characteristic of this Structuralist architectural concept, and at the same time its distinguishing mark in terms of building, is an arrangement of rooms both in equal elements within human comprehension and within a geometric roster. The architectonic form is determined by a communication net that covers the entire layout. The building, in this process, is considered as part of the entire urban structure and should contribute to the social or communicative contacts between the inhabitants or users of the building.

The ideas and concepts of Structuralism led in the 1960s to user participation in the process of planning and design. The

return to a consideration of human needs as a limitation to the Modern Movement was the starting point of this architectural movement. Future development will show to what extent the user is in a position to formulate his living and working conditions, with special consideration of the harmonious and human aspects.

A number of essential design principles based on the idea of Structuralism can be clearly distinguished in Piet Blom's individual projects. In the casbah in Hengelo and in the tree houses in Helmond, the "spatial organization is rejuvenated'' by the situation created by the new living units; "it adapts itself, and in the process rejuvenates the living conditions'' (1, p. 1,221). The single-family house is moved to the second floor, above ground, so that the "people who live in the town can make use of the space below their dwellings (on the ground floor, which is a part of space associated with the public road.'' A general and public zone of communication is offered on the ground floor. By diverse means, possibilities are created to permit the user to participate in the formation of his personal

environment or to allow him to create parts of that environment himself. The person living in the tree house is almost forced by the unconventional form of the rooms to make use of his own ideas to develop a new method of using the spaces provided, in the sense of "a speech for the defence against total welfare, and for a return to responsibility for one's own affairs.'' Another clearly visible objective is an addition of equal and geometric spatial elements. At the same time, the total layout remains dominant in the general appearance of the development, so that in the event of alterations (either by addition or by subtraction) the visual order remains undisturbed. These requirements follow from the thesis of the twin phenomena of "order and chaos.'' According to Blom, it is incorrect to assume that "spatial planning is required merely inside, and that external surfaces can be ordered two-dimensionally. Today this is an exercise in four dimensions. The third dimension is the vertical, and the fourth is the freedom for the change in time, which influences the entire plan'' (2, p. 1,222).

GENERAL PRINCIPLES

+The form (situation) of the town plan should be free and alterable, and it should be possible to change its function even after several years + (1, p. 1,221).

JUSTIFICATION

"The spatial organization of a city can adapt itself to a given situation, and can renew itself, and in the process it rejuvenates the living conditions" (1, p. 1,221).

Simple and unmistakable characteristics of the "dwelling place" (only a single identification of the dwelling "place" is possible) (1, p. 1,219).

Avoidance of an anonymous and unspecified "address" (1, p. 1,219).

+ *The resident shall be in evidence in the town and shall be able to express himself. Avoidance of a "passive" urban space* + *(1, p. 1,221).*

+ *The individual resident shall have the opportunity, within the structure of the town, "to do something with the urban space"* + *(1, p. 1,221).*

Possibility of adaptation of the "spatial organization" of the town:

*Neighborhood Unit Casbah
Hengelo, Netherlands
1972–73*

Unmistakable characteristics of the dwelling place, which result in identification with one's personal residential environment:

*Neighborhood Unit Casbah
Hengelo, Netherlands
1972–73*

Creating the potential for self-expression for the resident in "his" region of the town or dwelling:

*Neighborhood Unit Casbah
Hengelo, Netherlands
1972–73*

TOWN-PLANNING LEVEL

Division of the structure of the town into constant (dwelling) and flexible (public spaces in the town or streets) units. ". . . a roof between sky and town . . ." (1, p. 1,219).

Each dwelling unit has a "spatial" relationship, which is uniquely defined, to the units of the town structure that lie below it:

- Living above *A*
  (Dwellings above the laundry) or
- Living above *B*
  (Dwellings above the café), etc.

OBJECT LEVEL

An open-column grid at ground level permits the greatest possible variability and flexibility for "different situations in the future" (1, p. 1,222).

None of the dwelling units is an anonymous number; on the contrary, it stands in direct relation to the services of the publicly accessible town structure.

Direct allocation of private and official "open space" with the prospect of the mutual fertilization of the activities of individuals in the public space of the streets.

ZONE LEVEL

Addition of similar individual zones (dwelling units), that cover the actual "town structure" as an uninterrupted mosaic (for daylight).

A primary structure of ceiling (the lower boundary of the dwelling units) and floor (the land), together with side boundaries (the columns at ground level) encourages individual initiative.

TOWN-PLANNING LEVEL

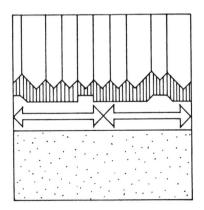

OBJECT LEVEL

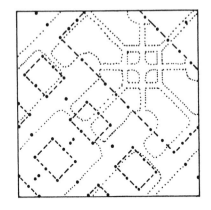

ZONE LEVEL

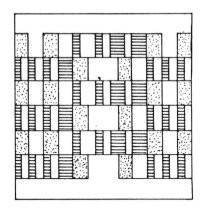

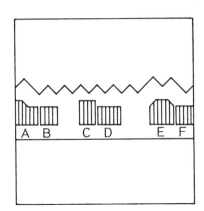

A B   C D   E F

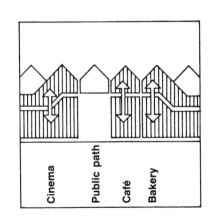

Cinema   Public path   Café   Bakery

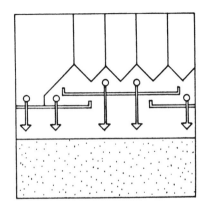

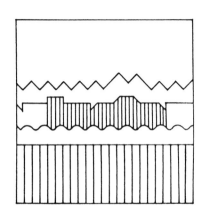

GENERAL PRINCIPLES

The creation of a differentiated sequence of spaces through the addition (repetition) of "economically conditioned" similar units (1, p. 1,221).

JUSTIFICATION

Avoidance of "repetition of forms devoid of comfort," monotonous spaces as plazas or streets, or sterile arrangements of buildings (1, p. 1,221).

Conscious striving for "great formal richness" (3, p. 1,227).

At the request of the citizens, a formal change in the "miserable condition of this town" (3, p. 1,227).

"The scale which the pedestrian (at ground level) encounters shall be human, that is, small" (3, p. 1,227).

+The magnificence of a building is less important than its human scale + (3, p. 1,225).

*Creation of differentiated sequences
of rooms to avoid "the repetition of
forms devoid of comfort," as shown
in the Neighborhood Unit Casbah,
Hengelo, Netherlands, 1972–73, illustrated earlier.*

*Creation of "great formal richness"
to change "the miserable condition
of the town":*

*Tree Houses and Central Meeting
Place
Helmond, Netherlands
1975–79*

*Restoration of the "human" scale
for pedestrians:*

*Tree Houses and Central Meeting
Place
Helmond, Netherlands
1975–79*

TOWN-PLANNING LEVEL

Creation of rooms through the differentiated use of roof elements, terraces, and courtyards.

OBJECT LEVEL

Characterization of differentiated situations in rooms through zones of darkness and light, which depend on the surfaces with buildings and without buildings.

ZONE LEVEL

Equal units of ground and their replacement units make it possible, by addition, to produce differentiated utilization (differentiated dwelling units).

Strong differentiation of the boundaries of the urban spaces and their components within a single layout.

A cube element aligned along its corner as an "unusual house form" and as a building form with many variations.

The use of unusual openings and window shapes promotes a formal richness with many variations of form both on the façade and on the boundaries of the rooms inside (wall surfaces).

Expression of small room units on the outside. This avoids long, straight stories that are out of scale with the general layout.

"Small room units" make it possible to "adapt" the design to existing small-scale buildings.

Clearly perceptible limitations of space from the perspective view of a pedestrian (horizontal and vertical through the structure of the tree houses). Expression of small and perceptible dimensions of buildings and rooms.

TOWN-PLANNING LEVEL
    OBJECT LEVEL
    ZONE LEVEL

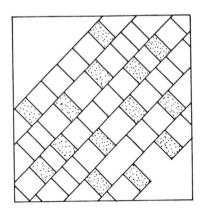 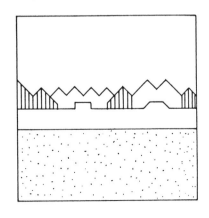 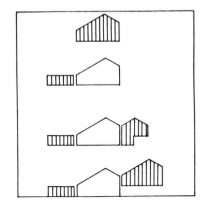

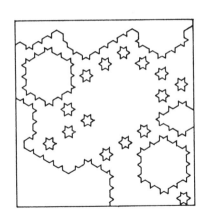 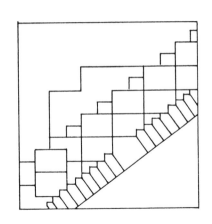 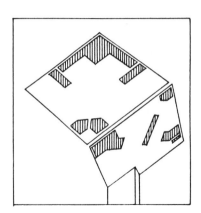

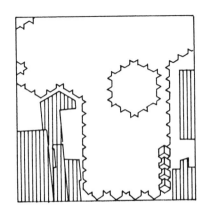 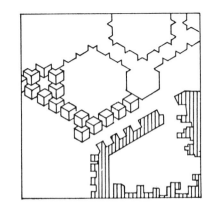 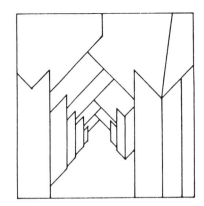

GENERAL PRINCIPLES	**JUSTIFICATION**
+The entire layout must be capable of expansion over a period of time, without substantial alteration of the overall appearance + (3, p. 1,225).	+Possibility of adaptation to new uses in the future + (3, p. 1,225).
"It should be possible, as the years progress, to fill gaps, reinterpret the layout, and correct human, urban, and noncommercial arrangements" in the assembly of buildings (3, p. 1,227).	"We must . . . arrive at a type of urban structure which allows enough room for a vibrant life, an urban structure in which the activities of the individual are revived" (2, p. 1,228).
Creation of differentiated and novel experiences of space (3, p. 1,227).	"Original, free fantasy shall be mobilized" for the utilization or arrangement of space; that is, "original interpretation is of decisive importance" (7, pp. 228–9).

The entire layout should be capable of development over a period of time, without alteration of its essential visual appearance:

Tree Houses and Central Meeting Place
Helmond, Netherlands
1975–79

"Arrangements which permit the filling of gaps, reinterpretation of the layout" over a period of years. "Capability for correcting human, urban, and noncommercial arrangements" over a period of years:

Tree Houses and Central Meeting Place
Helmond, Netherlands
1975–79

Differentiation of the orientation of individual rooms. New and unfamiliar room shapes for mobilizing original and free fantasy:

Tree Houses and Central Meeting Place
Helmond, Netherlands
1975–79

TOWN-PLANNING LEVEL	OBJECT LEVEL	ZONE LEVEL

Principle of the addition of identical units makes possible differentiated growth in stages.

1 = 1st segment of building development
2 = 2nd segment
3 = 3rd segment

"Building between sky and public street . . . as an urban variant of the house in the country" (3, p. 1,225).

Only the "columns" are fixed points in the public space of the street; the remaining space can be used and enjoyed for various purposes.

The existence of a roof makes it possible to use the space between the columns throughout the year as a public marketplace.

Rooms have differentiated relationships to the environment and differentiated shapes:

1 = "column"
2 = "street house"
3 = "sky house"
4 = "greenhouse"

Differentiation of the shape of the rooms within a single zone of the "tree house" (cube).

TOWN-PLANNING LEVEL   **OBJECT LEVEL**   **ZONE LEVEL**

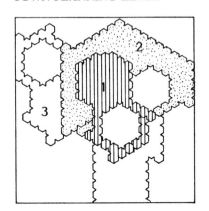

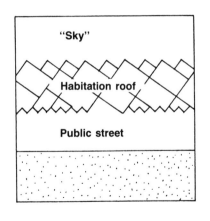

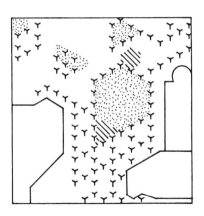

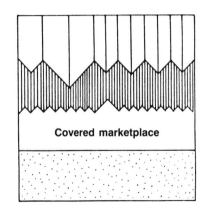

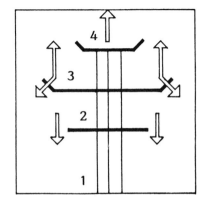

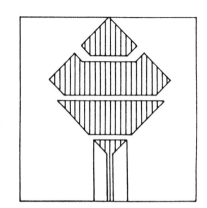

Herman Hertzberger belongs to the Structuralist group of architects. The essential goals of this group have already been briefly described in the section on Piet Blom.

A number of aspects of the Structuralist philosophy are realized in Hertzberger's buildings and projects. The inclusion of the design of the environment is a design feature that extends from housing (Diagoon Houses) through the workplace (Centraal Beheer) to retirement homes (De Drie Hoven). The façades and building panels of the Diagoon Houses can be designed or installed by the user himself after the fabric of the house has been completed. In the case of the office building Centraal Beheer, the offer of including the user in the design of the architectural environment goes even further: "The fabric is also the finished product"—this is the goal set in Hertzberger's design concept. This is intended to encourage and promote individual interior design of the working environment; since everybody creates his own personal working environment, the identification of the individual's zone—exemplified here by his workplace—is enhanced.

A further principle central to the Structuralist concept is the creation of social contacts; that is, the representation of the social structure of the city in the widest sense, which governs people living together in the same building. The retirement home De Drie Hoven offers a balanced hierarchy of communication zones. This structural organization of rooms in a building is modeled on the familiar forms of the city center, the town quarter, and the domestic neighborhood, and is delineated as spatial elements. The continuation of the creation of social contacts is one of the goals, so that the building is part of a net of the urban communication structure. In a modified form, the concept attempts to embrace the social contacts resulting from the public pedestrian paths to the building as an image of the urban structure.

The spatial organization resulting from the inclusion of "pedestrian paths" into the office building Centraal Beheer is supported by an appropriate design of that zone. The character of the "public space of the road" is created by the arrangement of a series of artifacts, as for example a church-tower clock, a telephone booth, a mailbox, a fire hydrant, or pedestrian paving.

The design of surfaces and workplaces used by individuals is intended to satisfy the human need for mutual information. The structure of the building develops from these considerations, and it makes possible vertical and horizontal communication through visual references and continuing spatial sequences. In accordance with the idea of Structuralism, the entire complex is the sum of small, individual units of space, which are geometrically and formally equal or similar.

In the design of the architectural unit, special importance attaches to the potential for multiple use. In consequence, the individual use of the various zones in Centraal Beheer is not specified but is left to future development. At the same time, Hertzberger adds these small, comprehensible units without specifying their use, in accordance with the demands of Structuralism: that is, "Things may only be big if they form a multiple of small units, because excess quickly creates disparity. By making everything too big, too

empty, and thereby remote . . ." architectural places and spaces become inhospitable and create user resistance (8, p. 21).

The concepts of Structuralism, and particularly the work of Hertzberger, resulted in the 1960s in the realization by architectonic means of participation problems, which had been discussed so often. The following examples show the extent to which the architect, through his work, can help with the solution of these problems.

GENERAL PRINCIPLES	JUSTIFICATION
". . . improvement of the living conditions and of the environment . . . leading to a human architecture" (9, p. 242). ". . . to offer the greatest possible potential for social contact" (10, p. 14).	+ A building should have a structure that facilitates social contacts, like the structure of the city + (10, p. 14).
+A building should be designed to accommodate the most diverse functions—in contrast to the "Garden City" and the "Modern" building. The four functions are: living, communication, work, and recreation + (6, p. 210).	The mixture of functions creates a social basis that contrasts with the separation of functions (6, p. 210).
+Creation of small and comprehensible units (in accordance with the human scale) + (8, p. 21).	"Things may only be big if they form a multiple of small units, because excess . . . creates disparity . . . and an inhospitable character" (8, p. 2).

". . . improvements of living conditions and of the environment":

Retirement Homes
De Drie Hoven
Amsterdam, Netherlands
1972–74

The social basis of the design of a building is to accommodate the most diverse functions:

Office Building, Centraal Beheer
Apeldoorn, Netherlands
1970–72

Creation of small comprehensible units:

Office Building, Centraal Beheer
Apeldoorn, Netherlands
1970–72

Herman Hertzberger **29**

TOWN-PLANNING LEVEL

+ The central communal space can be compared to the "center" of a city. + This means that it is accessible from the surrounding quarters and is laid out for public use as a "village square" (6, p. 14).

"Along the pedestrian paths in the complex of buildings there are many items of street furniture for public use" (6, p. 10).

". . . multiplicity built up from units that are themselves small . . ." takes account of the limited human capacity for comprehension (8, p. 21).

OBJECT LEVEL

+ The places where one meets on the stairs correspond to the town quarter + (6, p. 14).

Arrangement of public facilities on the ground floor: kiosk, kindergarten, shops, café, restaurant, library, etc.

Division of the buildings into distinct units for the uncomplicated orientation and comprehensible perception of the individual zones of a building complex.

ZONE LEVEL

The communal living room (for about 18 apartments) corresponds to the neighborhood of the town (10, p. 14).

Open workplaces provide the potential for "horizontal" and "vertical" communication.

The individual workplace is a "closed" unit that can easily be comprehended. It is joined to the general structure of the building through "public" zones.

TOWN-PLANNING LEVEL

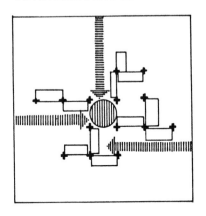

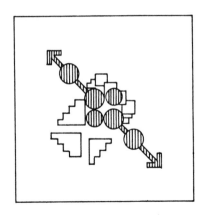

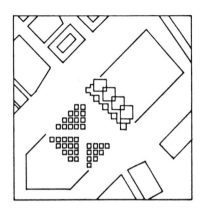

OBJECT LEVEL

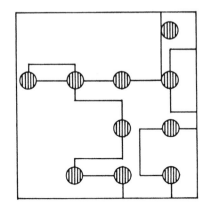

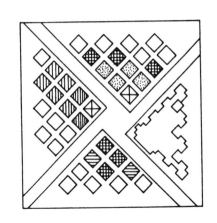

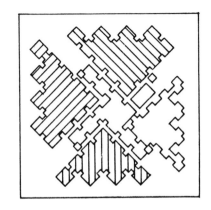

ZONE LEVEL

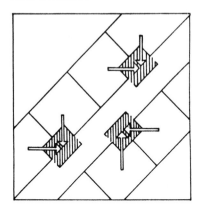

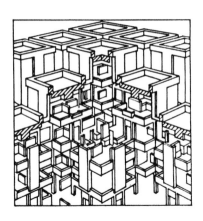

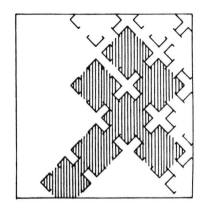

Herman Hertzberger **31**

GENERAL PRINCIPLES

+The boundary between the building and the public part of the urban structure should be abolished. The building should become part of the entire urban texture + (3, pp. 3 *et seq.*).

+ Development of structure and form, which can be developed further over a period of time. The form of the building is at all times incomplete, and it can, in different phases, be extended and/or reduced + (3, p. 12).

Making the construction visible and keeping the surfaces of the construction elements in an "unfinished" state (3, p. 15).

JUSTIFICATION

No distance or threshold should be placed between the architecture or the built substance, and the user. The environment thereby becomes accepted as something that exists as a matter of course and is both harmless and trustworthy + (3, p. 7).

Flexibility of the user surfaces after extension or reduction. In this process the inner function and organization are maintained.

For the clarification of possible future alterations, and for the stimulation and motivation of the user, to cooperate in the design of his environment (his workplace).

Removal of the boundary between the building and the structure of the city:

Office Building, Centraal Beheer Apeldoorn, Netherlands 1970–72

Development of structure and form, which can develop further over a period of time:

Office Building, Centraal Beheer Apeldoorn, Netherlands 1970–72

Creation of an image of the construction and the structure of the fabric for the stimulation of the individual fantasy of future users:

Retirement Homes, De Drie Hoven Amsterdam, Netherlands 1972–74

Herman Hertzberger   **33**

TOWN-PLANNING LEVEL

Existing pedestrian flow patterns are preserved as "public" paths in the building.

OBJECT LEVEL

The individual entrances and their adjacent entrance zones are carried into the building as "pedestrian paths" so that they have a continuation inside the building.

ZONE LEVEL

Integration of the interior and the exterior in each individual zone of the building.

Use of a cell structure so that, in the event of an extension or reduction of individual parts, the exterior and interior appearance of the basic structure remains essentially unaltered.

"Basic structure" and "interpretable zone." The basic structure corresponds to the construction and the arrangement of the supply systems. The interpretable zones can be utilized for various functions.

Variations for the use of the "primary building stones":

- Workplace
- Consultation
- Rest room
- Cafeteria, etc.

Clearly visible representation of the structure—for example, by emphasizing the ends of the beams in the central core.

The structural joints clearly visible on the façade.

TOWN-PLANNING LEVEL

OBJECT LEVEL

ZONE LEVEL

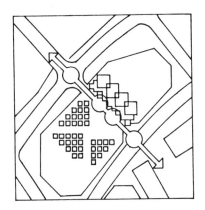

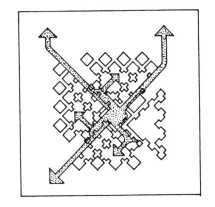

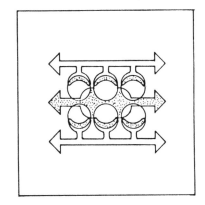

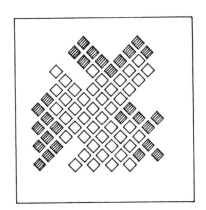

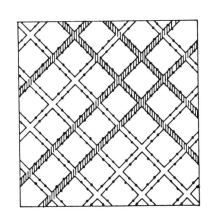

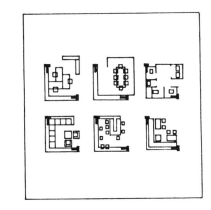

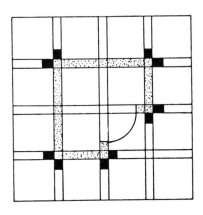

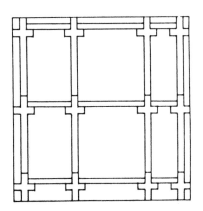

GENERAL PRINCIPLES	JUSTIFICATION
+The form shall not be neutral; on the contrary, it shall contain a multiplicity of offerings + (16, p. 145).	+. . . the form shall constantly call to mind living associations + (16, p. 145).
+The inhabitant (user) shall, as far as possible, make the decisions on his own environment + (16, p. 146).	+The user is more likely to identify with his environment if he is involved in the design process + (16, p. 146).
". . . architecture for people does not represent authority" (9, p. 242).	To avoid "architectural" authoritarianism one should strive, for example, "to create a music shop rather than a music temple" (15, p. 335).

Creation of a multiplicity of potential uses, in contrast to a "neutral" form:

*Retirement Homes, De Drie Hoven
Amsterdam, Netherlands
1972–74*

Offer of personal decision or personal design of the environment by the user:

*Office Building, Centraal Beheer
Apeldoorn, Netherlands
1970–72*

Creation of an "architecture for people":

*Music Center with Shopping Arcade
Utrecht, Netherlands
1976–78*

TOWN-PLANNING LEVEL

Provision of an "open-air layout" for the use of the inhabitants (users):

- Zoo for small animals
- Garden
- Leisure ground in conjunction with a public green belt.

Selection of small-scale urban structure for pedestrians, and continuation of the public spaces of the street within the building.

OBJECT LEVEL

Extensions of "pedestrian paths" for individual use and creation of a transition zone between the private space and the public street.

The fabric is also the finished building. This means that the actual character of the spaces will be determined in consultation with the user, or the user will design them himself. "Incompleteness of the building, greyness, bare concrete" (7, p. 211).

"The actual building of the music center is surrounded by shops, an information center, offices, and restaurants" (15, p. 335).

ZONE LEVEL

Provision of façades that give a potential for differentiated divisions, depending on the needs and wishes of the current users.

An unfinished design of space should encourage new uses. "Form evokes function" (16, p. 146).

". . . not a large hall for a foyer, but loosely combined units, which nevertheless form a coherent space" (8, p. 335).

TOWN-PLANNING LEVEL

OBJECT LEVEL

ZONE LEVEL

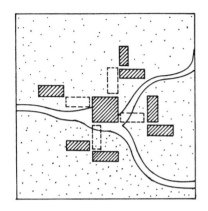

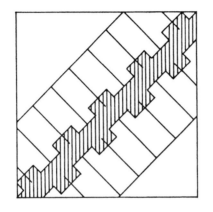

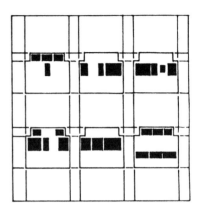

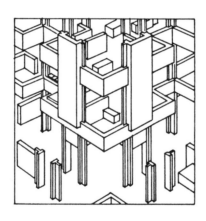

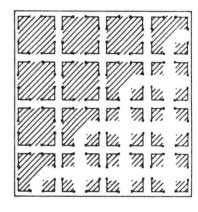

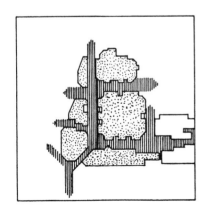

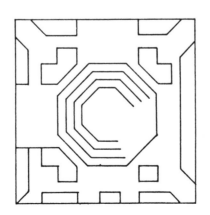

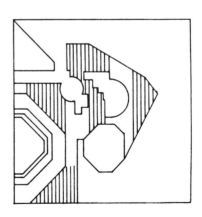

Herman Hertzberger **39**

Hans Hollein

"Man creates artificial situations. That is architecture. He determines the 'environment' in its widest sense by physically and psychologically repeating, transforming and extending his physical and psychological domain. To satisfy his needs and his wishes, he employs whatever means satisfy his needs and fulfill his wishes and dreams. . . . Architecture is a medium of communication" (7, p. 2).

With these few words, Hans Hollein outlines the task of architecture and the field of activity of the architect. Architecture is for him the transformation of an idea, using the "artistic" media provided by the technology of our century. The building is for him the result of wishes and thought processes translated into practice. To appreciate the essential aspects of Hollein's archi-

tecture, one must consider his change in emphasis from "meaning to effect." For him, architecture has an "effect." A building can accordingly be reduced to a carrier of information; that is, pure information between "sender" and "receiver" (7, p. 2). Thus, the Egyptian pyramids transmit a self-contained system of information; without it, their architecture cannot be spatially or physically experienced. According to Hollein, every element of our environment is an important carrier of information. Architecture is a medium of reciprocal information. Thus, a design or visual image does not depend on the state of our technology or contemporary culture but on the intellectual potential of "man himself." Accordingly, the visual image is created in the form of a carrier of information,

and it does not depend on function, constructional principles, or "structure."

Against this background, Hollein has developed a series of concepts, in which the medium of architecture becomes the transmitting element. In his capacity as a plastic artist, Hollein has transformed allegorical and metaphorical themes into spatial/visual situations. In his architectural projects, these goals were extended through the creation of specific impressions that form, space, or symbols make on people. The artistic nature of the architecture so created is emphasized partly by the use of costly materials and more generally by perfect finishes. The pursuit of the design idea to the perfection of every detail is of decisive significance in achieving the goal that Hollein has set himself in his work. In some of his projects, this comprehensive approach to architecture includes the design of the furniture.

The technically perfect construction of the built environment, which is a feature of the projects by Hollein discussed on the following pages, and its superposition with communicable information, are basically a continuation of the functionalist idea, to the extent that they deal with the finishing process of an architectural product. To achieve a built and physical architecture, Hollein shows an intense preoccupation with the quality of his spaces, and he regards the possibility of satisfying psychological and physiological needs as a precondition. "Rooms which have haptic, optical and acoustic qualities are more likely to retain information consciously, and they will also respond directly to subjective demands" (7, p. 2).

A genuine architecture of our time, according to Hollein, is in the process "of defining itself anew as a medium, and expanding its range of expression. . . . Everything is architecture" (7, p. 2). This definition also describes Hollein's field of activity, which extends from architecture via the plastic arts to literary works.

GENERAL PRINCIPLES	JUSTIFICATION
Provision of a neutral structure of space (16, p. 3).	Maintenance of flexibility "in the event of an alteration of functions, to arrange different, customer-oriented activities in the space reserved for customers ('in-coming and out-going business')" (16, pp. 3, 4).
"Architecture is ceremonially and ritually a medium of communication"; that is, "the object is given an additional dimension . . . corresponding to the demands of a structure that has a multiplicity of strata" (21, p. 3).	These "metaphorical" elements or "citations" shall awaken "associations with what is offered here" (16, p. 3).
Creation of a "multiplicity of strata also at the reception desk; that is, to create an ambience that is comprehensible from the various entrances, and that can be reciprocated. . ." (16, p. 3).	The architectural space should "not be allowed to slip into simple decoration or exhibition architecture" (16, p. 3).

Creation of a neutral structure of space:

Austrian Travel Bureau
Vienna, Austria
1976

Architecture as a medium of communication:

Austrian Travel Bureau
Vienna, Austria
1976

Creation of a "structure of many strata at the reception desk":

Austrian Travel Bureau
Vienna, Austria
1976

TOWN-PLANNING LEVEL	OBJECT LEVEL	ZONE LEVEL
	". . . great, comparatively neutral hall . . ." as architectural concept of space (16, p. 3).	". . . introduction of repetitive, exhangeable, and simple elements . . ." to support the character of a neutral hall: inserted columns and rudimentary partitions in the space used by the customers (16, p. 3).
	"A 'scenario' of iconographic, metaphorical, and associative elements . . ." as ". . . consciously inserted, significant objects placed in a definite order into their neutral space" (16, p. 3).	The scenario "palms," which associates the palms in the foreground with holidays and paradise (16, p. 3).
	"Quotations from the history of architecture": for example, the representation of palms copied from Nash's Royal Pavilion in Brighton, or the use of the type of hall used in Otto Wagner's Post Office Savings Bank in Vienna (16, p. 3).	"Modification or transformation" of the inserted elements; for example, by transformation of the material: • "Brass palms" • "Brass curtain" • "Part of a pyramid" • "Brass column" • "Marble seats."

TOWN-PLANNING LEVEL   **OBJECT LEVEL**   **ZONE LEVEL**

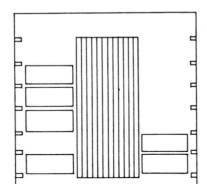
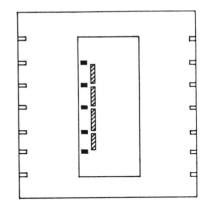

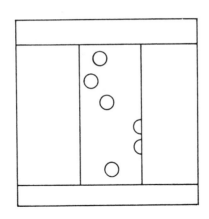
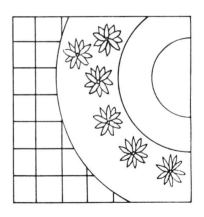

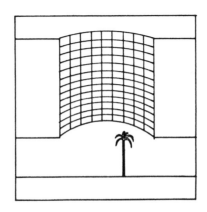

Hans Hollein   **45**

GENERAL PRINCIPLES	JUSTIFICATION
Representation of the division into a "neutral structured space" and the spatial elements finished for use (17).	Emphasis on the neutral structure of the space by accentuation of the independent built-in elements.
"Form as function, form creates function. Form is an integral part of the spiritual content" for the definition of the building (18, p. 1,590).	The form shall be used as the "medium for (spatial) communication." That is, it shall be possible, through the corresponding shape, to transmit certain information (21, p. 3).
+ Semiotic representation of functions . . . creation of associations through iconography + (9, p. 1).	+ Support for the medium of "architecture" as a means of communication + (12).

Division of the "neutral structure of the space" and of the spatial elements finished for use:

Austrian Travel Bureau
Vienna, Austria
1976

Architecture (form) as a medium for communication. Conveyance of information through the (architectural) shape:

Retti, shop for the sale of candles
Vienna, Austria
1964–65

Architectural form as a means for the "creation of associations through iconography":

Schullin, Jeweler's shop
Vienna, Austria
1972–74

TOWN-PLANNING LEVEL

OBJECT LEVEL

Superimposition of the primary geometry of the space by spatial borders that are differentiated and alterable. These additional boundaries of the space show at the same time the directions for movement to the different user zones.

ZONE LEVEL

Contrast between the orthogonal pattern on the floor and the "freeform" circular segments. These circular elements simultaneously emphasize the entrance zones by providing two-dimensional guidelines into the space.

"Semiological attitude of the architecture, a façade that is effective in the distance . . .

. . . and nearby" through the superimposition of a scale (12). The large-scale features of the form are effective from a distance, while the small-scale divisions created by the showcases convey information on the parts close by.

The form of the "portal should pass over into the inner space without a change of material . . . and thereby make a processional concept possible through height and movement" (5, p. 1).

"The means of the (architectural) communication are not applied to the surface, but are part of the architecture." "Liquid or fluid gold" is integrated into the ventilation elements as a contrast to the structural grid (17).

A close connection between decoration and function. "Architecture is semiotic, associative, ambivalent." "Strategic use of means; that is, exchange expensive components for those that cost less" (12 and 9, p. 1).

TOWN-PLANNING LEVEL   **OBJECT LEVEL**   **ZONE LEVEL**

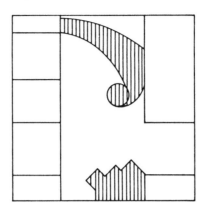 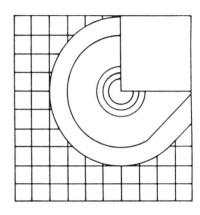

 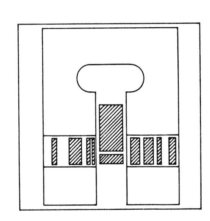 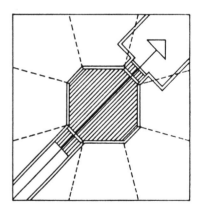

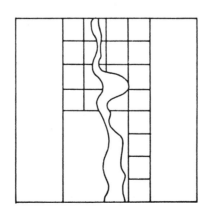 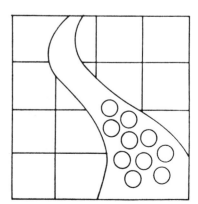

Isozaki was a pupil of and former collaborator with Kenzo Tange, and his first buildings and projects show the influence of the ideas of Metabolism. Starting from utopias for megastructures for future cities (Plan of Tokyo with Kenzo Tange—1960, Spatial City—1960, and City in the Air—1962), he transformed the traditional model and form of Japanese wooden architecture. In the Library of Oita (1965), for example, the column/beam theme becomes the basic structural element of his architecture. The fundamental elements of his architectural spaces are based on the elementary stereometric forms of the cube, the parallelepiped, and the cylinder, as well as the so-called Monroe curve.

With the new building for the Takasaki Museum (Gumma, 1974), Isozaki outgrew the ideas of Metabolism and at the same time commenced a new and individual approach. In Japan and in international discussion, the belief in technical progress and economic growth has gradually faded and with it the inducement to the Metabolists' development of grandiose, technically based utopias (16, p. 205). The high point and, for the time being, the end of these visions, was reached with the design of the Festival Plaza of Expo '70 in Osaka by Kenzo Tange, Isozaki, Kurokawa, and others. In spite of the abundance of information on the future problems of people living together in large numbers, Isozaki lacked unequivocal models (16, p. 209) for the continuation of his Metabolic visions. Isozaki attempted comparisons with other civilizations, such as those of the Renaissance and the Baroque, whose styles had been determined by relatively firm conceptions of the world, and which consequently developed an unequivocal architectural style. From this insight, Isozaki developed new and individual goals.

Starting with the rich repertoire of architectural forms derived from the history of both Western and Eastern architecture—Palladio, Ledoux, Bruno Taut, and the Japanese temples and shrines, such as those of Ise and Izumo— Isozaki developed his own concept for the design of buildings, which he called "maniera." By "maniera" he means a manner, in the sense of Mannerism, as the basis for architectural design. He attempts to adopt the ideas and concepts of this epoch, whose style is intermediate between that of the Renaissance and the Baroque, to interpret it anew, and to realize it in his buildings. Starting with the design principle of adding equal, geometric units (for example, in the Takasaki Museum, cubic units measuring 12.0 m by 12.0 m), he follows this with a second design principle whereby, in a multiplicity of ways, alternative elements are introduced; the major units, however, remain as the primary structure (15, p. 100). For the realization of these design principles, Isozaki employs a series of different means: for example, the gradual fading of a geometric grid, or the employment of picturesque elements, such as diago-nal lines drawn across walls and ceilings, which begin to counter-act the unity of the orthogonal space, as well as the insertion of plastic elements to alter the per-ceptible geometry of the space by perspective foreshortenings (entrance hall of the Takasaki Museum).

Isozaki himself describes the historic Mannerism of the six-teenth century as the source of his inspiration (15, p. 100). A fur-ther source for his designs was provided by the concepts of the revolutionary architecture of Ledoux and Boullée (13). From this background Isozaki approaches the ideas of Rational-ism, without succumbing to the danger of a schematic restructur-ing of the environment with ster-eometrically based architectural elements. The realization of his architectural goals has essentially been influenced by a series of distinct "manners." At the end of the 1960s, Isozaki had already formulated a series of methods ("maniera"), on which his var-ious architectural designs are based. The following analysis presents some of these essential "design methods."

GENERAL PRINCIPLES	JUSTIFICATION
+Assembly of the body of the building from clear geometric spatial elements, and their transformation through separation or segmentation (Method of Slicing) + (7, p. 24).	To emphasize and characterize the "finiteness" of the spatial elements, parts of them are clearly "cut" or "separated." The clear geometry demands "finiteness" (7, p. 24).
+Clear differentiation from the structure of the surrounding space, and separation of the interior from the exterior space (Method of Packaging) + (7, p. 25).	+To create "heterogeneous" (differentiated and artificial) spaces, a clear separation, which goes beyond the purely physical membrane, is necessary. (7, p. 25).
+Architectural form shall be developed as a medium for reciprocal information (communication) (Method of Response) + (7, p. 25).	For the creation and clarification of "fluid transitions" of information between users and contemporary architecture.

Assembly of the body of the building from clear geometric spatial elements, and their transformation through "slicing":

*Medical Hall
Oita, Japan
1970–72*

Separation of interior space from exterior space:

*Fukuoka Mutual Bank
Fukuoka, Japan
1968–71*

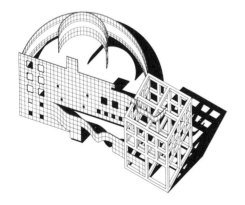

Architectural form as a medium of reciprocal communication:

*Town Hall
Kamioka, Japan
1978–79*

TOWN-PLANNING LEVEL

The body of the building is assembled from a series of clear geometric units. In plan or in section, these appear as "sliced" spatial forms.

OBJECT LEVEL

Addition of clear geometric surfaces to create an overall plan that depends on the chosen spatial elements and their transformation.

ZONE LEVEL

The cube as an element in an additive spatial body, and a boundary in space through "slicing."

The body of the building does not relate to the surrounding buildings. The mass of the building appears as an isolated element in the texture of the city, or it may stand in contrast to the existing situation.

Combination of the body of the building with simple and clear geometric space units. The overall shape remains clearly visible. Renunciation of many, or of large, exterior openings.

"Packed space" without reference to the preexisting environment.

The entrance zone shall be characterized by "mobile" spatial forms to contrast with the rigidly geometric character of the building body in general. "Soft" space forms contribute to a reduction of the threshold between citizen and administration, or between building and user.

"Swinging" spatial shapes in contrast to hard and unwelcoming plane space boundaries.

ARCHITECTURAL CHARACTERISTICS

TOWN-PLANNING LEVEL

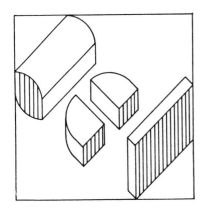

OBJECT LEVEL

ZONE LEVEL

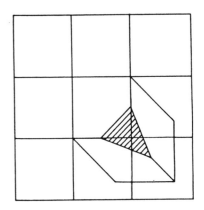

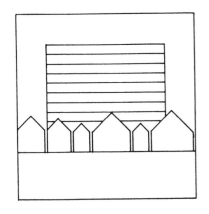

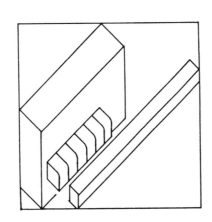

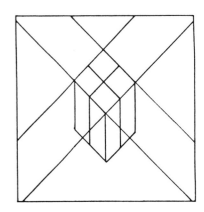

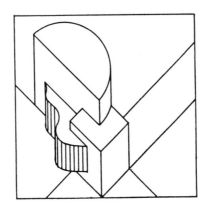

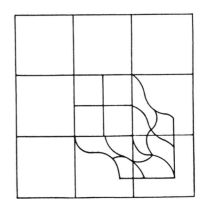

GENERAL PRINCIPLES

+ Arrangement of objects in space according to individual and symbolic significance. The structure of these objects does not depend on their constructional or functional associations (Method of Chessman) + (7, p. 24).

+ "Creation of spaces" through the addition of "growth" from neutral basic units, and their "infinite" subdivision of "superimposition" (Manner of Amplification) + (16, p. 209).

+ Interference and interruption of a clear and unequivocal system of order (Manner of Maniera) + (10, p. 37 and 16, p. 211).

JUSTIFICATION

Elements ("key elements") of architecture shall possess an "allegorical" expression (7, p. 24).

+ Through the use of such neutral basic units (spaces), the architectural space recedes in importance compared with the elements in this space + (10, p. 37).

Clarification of the geometric "rules" and emphasis on the "addition" through interfering elements. The unequivocal system is interrupted, and the relationships between individual objects become ambiguous (10, p. 37).

Arrangement of objects in space with symbolic significance:

*Fukuoka Mutual Bank
Tokyo, Japan
1970–71*

Creation of space through addition and growth:

*Modern Art Museum
Takasaki (Gumma), Japan
1971–75*

Interference with the spatial situation through a superimposed system of order:

*Modern Art Museum
Takasaki (Gumma), Japan
1971–75*

Arata Isozaki **57**

TOWN-PLANNING LEVEL

OBJECT LEVEL

The open and closed elements of the façade form a flourish to give an individual character and symbol to a particular institution.

ZONE LEVEL

Generation and presentation of architectural elements with symbolic significance, analogous to the significance of chess pieces and their position on the chess board. + (7, p. 24).

The entire volume of the space is composed of individual cubic frames. This structure is visible outside and inside, and it characterizes the entire layout.

The dimensioning and the subdivision of the basic units are visible and are continued in the façade and in the floor surface.

The "cube" is the basic unit, and it forms the primary structure; that is, it forms the actual space. "Continuation or growth" through "division of cells" and through addition (3, p. 37).

"The introduction of a new axis reveals the arrangement of the individual cubes" and characterizes, for example, an entrance zone as a special part (10, p. 37).

Emphasis on interference through the superimposition of the basic structure (in plan as a surface of water) with a skewed arrangement of the body of the building in the spaces at the higher levels.

Transformation of the impression of the space through a "built-in" perspective, analogous to a spatial illusion as a superimposition and emphasis on two separate design principles.

TOWN-PLANNING LEVEL   **OBJECT LEVEL**   **ZONE LEVEL**

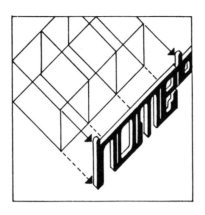 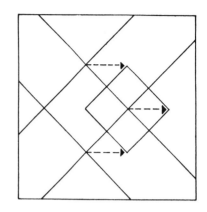

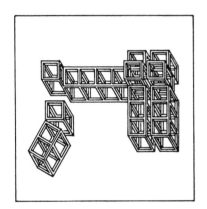 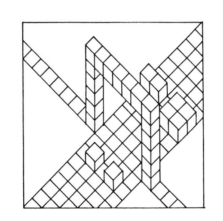 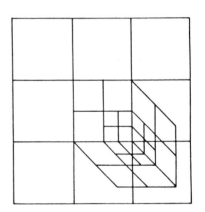

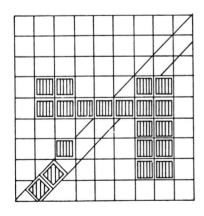 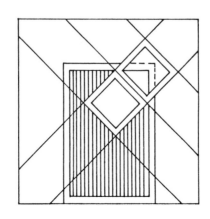 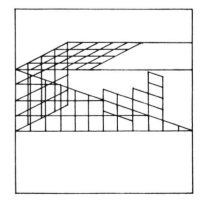

GENERAL MAXIMS	JUSTIFICATION
+ Unequivocal representation and emphasis on ''artificial spaces in plan and in elevation'' through the cube (The Metaphor of the Cube) + (11, p. 62).	+ The cube appears unnatural and is consequently installed as a ''symbol of artificiality'' + (11, p. 62).
+ Creation of spatial multiplicity and differentiated formation of spaces (Method of Projection) + (7, p. 24).	Portrayal of differentiated impressions of space. Creation of real and illusory impressions of space (7, p. 24).
Clear presentation of cubes of equal significance as the primary structure (16, p. 213).	The entire envelope of space appears to have equal significance because of the emphasis on the neutral structure of the cubes.

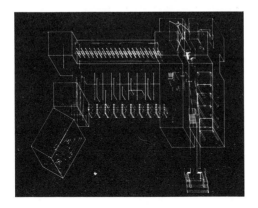

Presentation of and emphasis on artificial spaces:

*Modern Art Museum
Takasaki (Gumma), Japan
1971–75*

Creation of spatial multiplicity:

*(left): Fukuoka Mutual Bank
Oita, Japan
1966–67;
(right): Modern Art Museum
Takasaki (Gumma), Japan
1971–75*

Cubes as primary design elements:

*Modern Art Museum
Takasaki (Gumma), Japan
1971–75*

Arata Isozaki **61**

TOWN-PLANNING LEVEL

+ Artificial cube-shaped frames pile themselves up across the landscape and mark out a three-dimensional (exhibition) space. Emphasis on the artificiality of architecture as opposed to the natural landscape + (11, p. 53).

Change and counterpart of square and cube with 45° angles in the free space.

OBJECT LEVEL

"Marble steps, as for a temple, penetrate" (as an artificial element) the primary structure of the cubes. Emphasis on the artificiality of the individual architectural elements (16, p. 201).

Alienation of the space boundaries through projection of the edges of the cube over the wall and the ceiling. The original geometry is cancelled and creates new directions in space.

"Horizontal and vertical elements appear to be functionally equivalent." The edge of the roof, the columns, and the junction with the floor are developed equally without differentiation. (16, p. 212).

ZONE LEVEL

"The cube appears seldom in nature; it is a symbol for artificiality and can therefore easily be used as a metaphor for the 'artificial'" (11, p. 62).

"The horizontal and vertical boundaries of space become of equal value; the feeling of heaviness gives way before the neutral and alien spatial envelope" (16, p. 211).

There is no formal differentiation between the load-bearing and the non–load-bearing elements (columns and window surfaces). All elements continue the geometry of the cubes.

TOWN-PLANNING LEVEL

OBJECT LEVEL

ZONE LEVEL

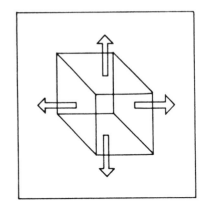

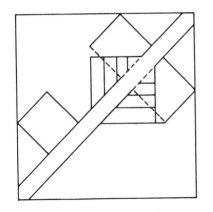

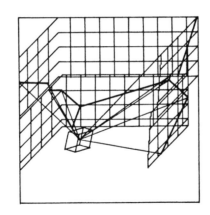

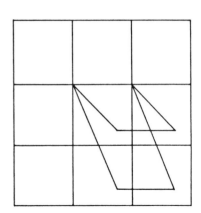

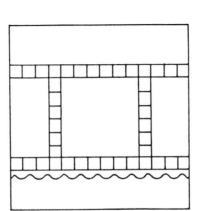

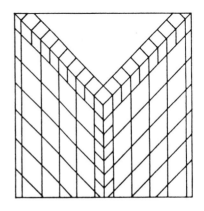

Louis Kahn

The international architecture of the end of the 1960s was influenced by many different versions and imitations of the International Style. Starting with the pioneers of the Modern Movement, such as Mies van der Rohe, Le Corbusier, and others, countless adaptations were produced (as for example the Formalism movement in the United States), which differed from one another only in their vocabulary of forms, too numerous for classification. It was at that time that Louis Kahn finished the Richards Medical Research Center in Philadelphia. The subsequent development of architectural trends shows that this project was a new starting point for the further discussion of architecture.

In the Medical Research Center, Kahn reinterpreted an essen-

tial aspect of design by his definition of "serving" and "served" space. In his discussion of the plan he returned to the tradition of the Beaux Arts. This tradition in his work "provided a formal and ideological basis, from which a master of a new architecture could find his personal style" (6, p. 167). With his concept of vertical brick towers and the associated floors, he reestablished a connection with the architectural concepts of the nineteenth century (which had been consciously broken by the Modern Movement), "without in any way sacrificing the achievements of the Modern Movement" (6, p. 168).

For Kahn, architecture begins "where the function has already been clearly established. At this stage the essence of the spaces

themselves reveals itself to the soul, and when their function has been properly understood, the spaces created fulfill a deep psychological need" (12, p. 239). For the activity of design, and for the design itself, this means that "before the design, before the actual creation of spaces," there was already in existence "a vision with its own incontestable qualities" (12, p. 209). For Kahn, design means giving presence to this vision, taking into account the laws of physics, so that the essence of the space and its creation "become one" (12, p. 209). According to Joedicke, Kahn distinguishes between two aspects of this process: "On the one hand, the comprehension of the general character of a thing, the essence of the thing itself, which for him is a generally valid truth, objective and generally applicable; and on the other hand the design, the translation of this generally valid piece of knowledge into a definite form, which can be further developed in the drawings'' (9, p. 122).

In addition to these frequently quoted statements, Kahn also made concrete assertions about the design of architectural spaces. For him, a space was ''not a space if one cannot understand how it was created'' (12, p. 246). The construction, or the ''process of fabrication'' of the elements that form the space, must be clearly readable, taking into particular account the properties of the materials. One particular concern is for the natural lighting of a space: ''I find that natural light gives a room its essence, its character, its feeling'' (12, p. 246). A space without natural light is for him not a space at all, because ''while the purpose of the space can be defined, its character cannot be defined.'' Consequently a building ''may have a very noble or a very low character, and in both cases it may function quite satisfactorily'' (12, p. 238).

With his thoughts on architectural spaces, often expressed in philosophical terms, and on the possibility of their realization, as well as a multitude of realized ideas in his international projects, Louis Kahn was a pathfinder of the architectural movement of the 1970s. In a series of discussions on the conditions and consequences of architecture as a medium for shaping the environment, Kahn reawakened our consciousness to the most diverse interrelationships. The world of ideas in Robert Venturi's first projects is unmistakably derived from Louis Kahn's thoughts.

Constants in the architecture of Louis Kahn, according to Giurgola and Mehta (5):
1. Composition and integrity of a "building" (5, p. 180).

LOUIS KAHN

GENERAL PRINCIPLES

Articulation of the body of the building through differentiation between "serving" and "served" spaces or floors (5, p. 181).

+ Integration of construction and space. A space only becomes a space when its construction is visible + (5, p. 66 *et seq.*).

+ A space should be an offer for use, without predetermining any specific use + (12, p. 237).

JUSTIFICATION

+ For the clarification of the character and the "essence" of individual spatial elements in the plan and the third dimension. +

+ The actual space is created through its construction + (5, p. 66).

"The room itself should stimulate a use"—separation of function and spatial character (12, p. 237).

Articulation of the body of the building into "serving" and "served" spaces:

Richards Medical Center
Philadelphia, PA
1957–61

Integration of construction and space. Making the construction visible:

Salk Institute for Biological Research
La Jolla, CA
1959–65

The space as an offer for different uses:

Student Residences, Bryn Mawr College
Bryn Mawr, PA
1960–65

TOWN-PLANNING LEVEL

Clear emphasis on the "serving" spaces (the supply towers, *1*) and the "served" spaces (the laboratory floors, *2*).

OBJECT LEVEL

The addition of the "serving" and the "served" elements to the structure of a plan, which is capable of performing the actual functions fully. An essential element is the arrangement or addition of equal elements to form a plan.

ZONE LEVEL

Arrangement of unpartitioned (flexible and variable) floor surfaces, and provision of specific vertical supply elements.

The piling up of alternate installations—"spaces" and independent floor surfaces.

The horizontal supply from the service floors creates the potential for large and coherent floor surfaces. These surfaces are uninterrupted by any fixed points and are limited only by the components of the structure.

Each space and each possible utilization are portrayed as independent spaces in the mass of the building.

Equal volumes of space are offered to the different activities.

A space can be defined or used as an entrance zone through the association of a few elements. This entrance zone is developed as the central traffic intersection.

TOWN-PLANNING LEVEL

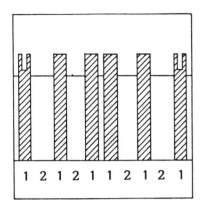

OBJECT LEVEL

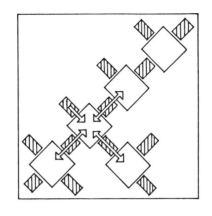

ZONE LEVEL

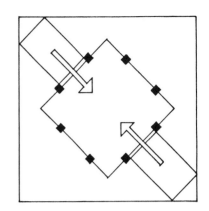

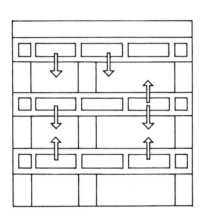

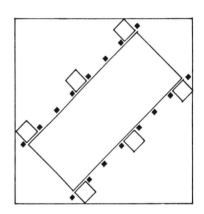

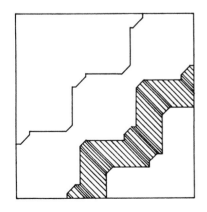

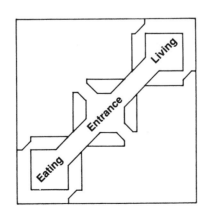

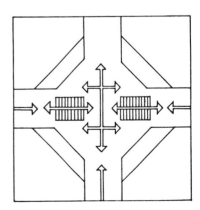

2. "Respect for the material" (5, p. 185).

LOUIS KAHN

GENERAL PRINCIPLES

Harmony between material, form, and fabrication process. The design should "consider the laws to which materials conform" (5, p. 186).

JUSTIFICATION

+ Representation of the construction principles to restore the relationship between man and nature (elucidation of natural laws) + (5, p. 185).

"The space must clearly show how it has been built." Construction-material properties of the envelope around the space should be clearly visible (12, p. 237).

"Space is not space, unless one can comprehend how it was made." In contrast to the "room" and the floor surface (for example, in the work of Mies van der Rohe) (12, p. 246).

+ Limitation to one or a few materials + (12, p. 228).

+ One should strive for structural order by limiting oneself to a few materials and to constructional principles that apply specifically to those materials + (12, p. 228).

Harmony between material, form, and fabrication process:

Indian Staff College
Ahmedabad, India
1963

"The space must clearly show how it has been built":

Richards Medical Center
Philadelphia, PA
1957–61

Limitation of the number of materials employed:

Indian Staff College
Ahmedabad, India
1963

TOWN-PLANNING LEVEL

OBJECT LEVEL

Articulation of the surfaces that limit the space (slabs of brickwork) by overemphasized brick arches.

ZONE LEVEL

"It is concerned with the glorification of two materials." Clear illustration of the lines of force, which are related to the different properties of the materials (brickwork and reinforced concrete (12, p. 229).

Accentuation of the columns at third points, which act as space-emphasizing elements in conjunction with the "serving" elements of the supply ducts.

To emphasize the creation of the space, essential construction elements and details were deliberately left visible or emphasized through their plasticity or surface texture.

The choice of brickwork as a material was an attempt to create unity ("harmony") between the building and the landscape through its constructional character—that is, its color and its surface texture.

The creation of space and the design of the building fabric are reduced to brickwork and reinforced concrete. Limitation to a few space-forming elements, such as columns, solid slabs, and slabs with openings.

Strong emphasis on the brick arches, through clear presentation of the construction principles that are determined by the nature of the materials. Reduction to one material: brickwork and its numerous construction methods.

TOWN-PLANNING LEVEL   **OBJECT LEVEL**   **ZONE LEVEL**

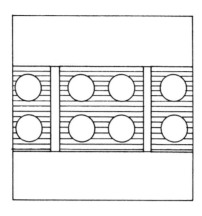

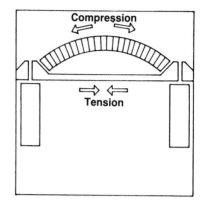

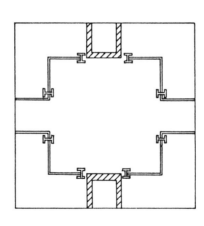

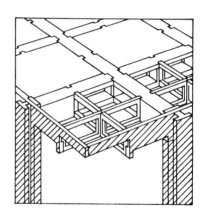

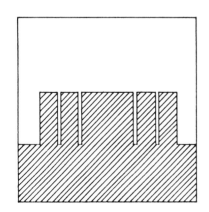

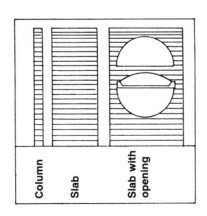

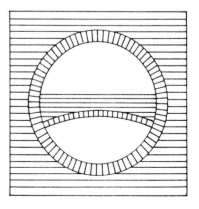

3. *"The individual space as the basic element of architecture; the plan as a union of spaces"* (5, p. 188).

LOUIS KAHN

GENERAL PRINCIPLES	JUSTIFICATION
+The plan is a union of spaces—that is, a composition of different spatial elements (5, p. 188).	+The single space, the single "room," is the basic unit of architectural design +. Emphasis on and clear presentation of this fundamental unit (5, p. 189).
+Determination of the form of a space in accordance with its character +. Finding the form is the result of a creative act (5, pp. 188, 221).	+Definition of the character of the architectural space (5, p. 189).
"Architecture begins when the functional requirements . . . have already been thoroughly comprehended . . ." (12, p. 239). Apart from the purely functional aspects, the architectural means selected must also satisfy other needs.	+Spaces must also gratify psychological requirements + (12, p. 239).

Plan as composition of different spatial elements:

*Government Offices
Dacca, Bangladesh
1973*

Development of form from the character of a space:

*Indian Staff College
Ahmedabad, India
1963*

Satisfaction of needs by architectural means:

*Student Residence, Bryn Mawr College
Bryn Mawr, PA
1960–65*

Louis Kahn **75**

TOWN-PLANNING LEVEL

Addition of individual "space complexes" to form an ordered general layout. Each "unit element" remains readable and is an essential part of the desired order.

OBJECT LEVEL

Addition of different space elements within the plan. The principle of the order is the grouping around a "central space" or about an axis of symmetry.

ZONE LEVEL

Addition of different units to form a single space. Emphasis on a clear and strong geometry for the unit element.

Arrangement of individual units to make the greatest possible use of the prevailing winds, and arrangement of the individual shapes to achieve the best sunshading possible.

The "residence" is a community whose rooms are arranged as a group around a central hall. The "essence" of the community lies in the individual living rooms. The shape of the hall is determined by the direction of the wind and the surfaces created by the shadows.

Transmission of the feeling of living together in a community, and being made to feel at home, by identification of one's "living quarters," as for example a "living room," a "dining room," a "bedroom," and an "entrance" to the building.

Equipment of the "residential zone" with typical living-room accessories: fireplace, seats arranged in a group, seats arranged in a recess, a dresser, and subdued lighting.

TOWN-PLANNING

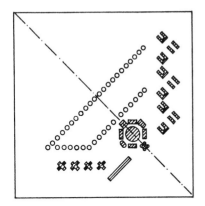

OBJECT LEVEL

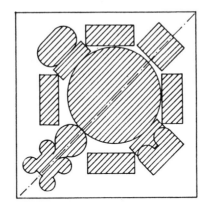

ZONE LEVEL

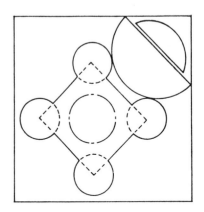

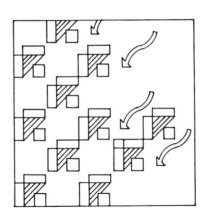

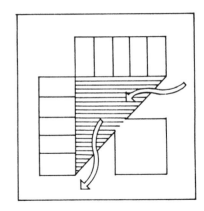

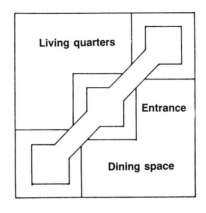

Living quarters

Entrance

Dining space

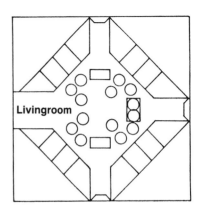

Livingroom

4. "*Light as a factor determining construction*" (5, p. 189).

LOUIS KAHN

GENERAL PRINCIPLES

+ Determination of the identity of a room through its natural light + (5, p. 199).

"The construction distributes the light." The construction should determine how light enters a room (12, p. 246).

+ As far as possible, illuminate a room with natural light + (12, p. 247).

JUSTIFICATION

The structure of the plan should show where there is light and where there is no light. Natural light produces a multitude of different spatial characteristics.

". . . natural light gives the room its character, its mood" (12, p. 246).

Artificially lit rooms do not have an independent existence or their own character.

Identity of a room through natural light:

Student Residence, Bryn Mawr College
Bryn Mawr, PA
1960–65

The construction dispenses the light:

Kimbell Museum of Fine Art
Fort Worth, TX
1967–72

Comprehensive illumination of a space with natural light:

Richards Medical Center
Philadelphia, PA
1957–61

Louis Kahn   **79**

TOWN-PLANNING LEVEL

OBJECT LEVEL

Emphasis on the inner zones through natural light. When walking through the rooms, differentiation between light and dark zones. Vertical illumination supports the perception of the third dimension.

ZONE LEVEL

A system of "reflectors" makes it possible to produce specific illumination of parts of a space—for example, emphasis on a particular function, such as the entrance zone, as an element of communication. Gradation of the illuminance by varying the direction of the light.

Supplementation of normal light with "green" light through the arrangement of "light courts" covered with plants.

Transformation of normal daylight into "silvery" light, which is received from the sky through horizontal windows and reflected by mirrors. The character of the space is determined by the mode of entry of the light (its angle of reflection).

Arrangement of the individual floor spaces with consideration of optimal daylight. All parts of the space receive the same illuminance. The only change results from the natural diurnal variation of daylight.

Reduction of the construction and service elements to a minimum to allow the greatest possible surface area for glazing.

TOWN-PLANNING LEVEL **OBJECT LEVEL** **ZONE LEVEL**

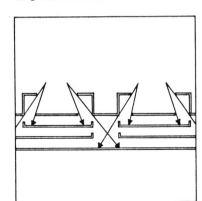
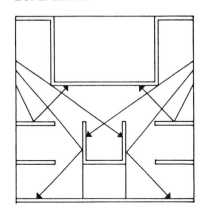

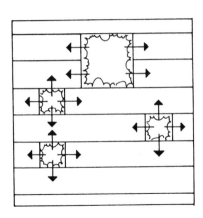
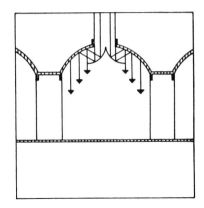

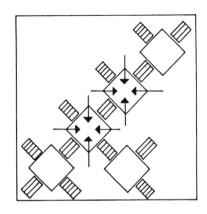
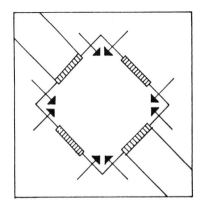

5. "Connections for creative architecture (1, p. 191).

LOUIS KAHN

GENERAL PRINCIPLES

+Creation of connections between spaces through the structure + (5, p. 19).

+Avoidance of sharp divisions of spaces through additional spatial elements, such as entrance halls or connecting rooms. The perception of space should proceed with continuity + (5, p. 192).

Direct and immediate connection of the individual volumes of the space (5, p. 192).

JUSTIFICATION

+Avoidance of arbitrary openings or additional spatial elements, such as corridors, if one can organize the structure so that the openings between two elements create the necessary connection + (5, p. 191).

+No walking backward and forward, but an interconnection of the individual volumes constituting the space. Enhancement of the spatial experience + (5, p. 192).

+Maintenance and enhancement of each individual element with regard to "the independent structural integrity" that is appropriate to each element + (5, p. 192).

Creation of connections between spaces through the structure, as shown in the Richards Medical Center, illustrated earlier.

Direct transition from one element of the space to the next:

Student Residence, Bryn Mawr College
Bryn Mawr, PA
1960—65

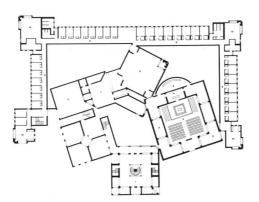

Placement of the individual units of the space in rows next to one another without an entrance hall:

Convent for Dominican Nuns
Media, PA
1965, Project

TOWN-PLANNING LEVEL	OBJECT LEVEL	ZONE LEVEL
	Displacement of spaces from the axis, to create a "natural" place for the door openings. Centrifugal arrangement of the individual domains around an entrance zone (5, p. 192).	
	Spatial connection between the unit spaces (parallelepipeds) through the intersection of the communicating edges. In this zone there are compelling locations for the entrances.	Vertical opening elements in the entrance hall as a connection between the spaces at the levels of the various stories.
	Direct connection of the individual spaces. The total freedom of the orientation of the spaces makes possible a direct relation of the individual spaces to one another. The architectural order is maintained by the environment.	The entrance system is subordinated to the geometric order of the individual spaces and loses its identity as a system. The individual spaces are placed in front.

TOWN-PLANNING LEVEL   **OBJECT LEVEL**   **ZONE LEVEL**

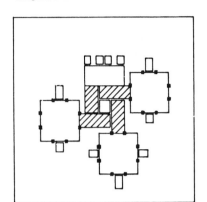

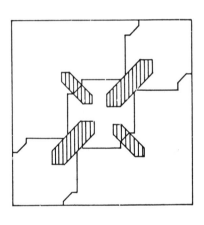

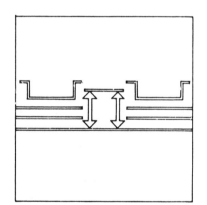

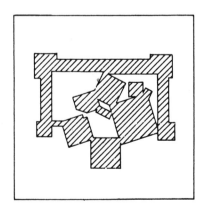

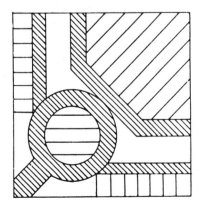

Charles Moore

At the beginning of the 1960s a project started north of San Francisco, which intimated the beginning of a new discussion on the content and significance of architecture: the Sea Ranch of Charles Moore. In this project a tradition in domestic construction, which has never been interrupted on the American west coast, is continued in a new form. Externally, this architecture is marked by the traditional design principles of the barn. Internally, new and very precise concepts of space are created: geometric figures produce a formal grid in plan; adjustable built-in units create a bond from room to room; and the form of the construction details is simplified as much as possible (18, p. 1154). Moore took as his model

the historic architecture of the American barns and the early farmhouses of the east coast, for which he had a particular preference.

In going back to these historical models, Moore participated in a development that made a decisive contribution to the discussion of architecture at the end of the 1970s. Charles Jencks coined the term "Postmodern" for this type of architecture. The representatives of this movement—especially in the United States and in England—have violently criticized the lack of expression and significance in Modern architecture. "Their target was the lack of symbolism of Modern architecture, its anonymity and the reduction of its expression to

one of technical functionalism as, supposedly, the only aim of design" (9, p. 192).

Charles Moore began to search for new forms and principles, in order to develop an architecture with universally intelligible metaphors. Moore formulated his requirements for a "significant" architecture and for "the creation of places" in five principles (17, p. 12 *et seq.*):

Principle 1: If we are to devote our lives to making buildings, we have to believe that they are worth it, that they live and speak (of themselves, and the people who made them and thus inhabit them), and can receive investments of energy and care from their inhabitants, and can store those investments, and return them augmented, bread cast on the water come back as club sandwiches.

Principle 2: If buildings are to speak, they must have freedom of speech. It seems to me that one of the most serious dangers to architecture is that people may just lose interest in it; the number of things buildings have in this half century been allowed to say has so diminished that there is little chance for surprise or wonder. If architecture is to survive in the human consciousness, then the things buildings can say, be they wistful or wise or powerful or gentle or heretical or silly, have to respond to the wide range of human feelings.

Principle 3: Buildings must be inhabitable by the bodies, minds, and memories of humankind. The urge to dwell, to inhabit, enhance, and protect a piece of the world, to fashion an inside and to distinguish it from the outside, is one of the basic human drives, but it has by now been so often thwarted that the act often requires help, and surrogates which can stand upright (like chimneys or columns) or grow and flourish (like plants) or move and dance

(like light) can act as important allies of inhabitation.

Principle 4: For us each to feel at the center of our universe, we need to measure and describe points in space as people used to do—in terms of ourselves, not of the precise but meaningless relations of, for instance, Cartesian coordinates or "rational" geometries. Soon after our birth we arrive at a sense of front and back, left and right, up, down, and center, which are so strong that we can and do assign moral significance to them. Our architecture needs to remember them, too, so that we can feel with our whole bodies the significance of where we are, not just see it with our eyes or reason it out in our minds.

Principle 5: The spaces we feel, the shapes we see, and the ways we move in buildings should assist the human memory in reconstructing connections through space and time. Half a century ago, those passages of the mind seemed oppressive, and full of cobwebs, and much effort went to cleaning them out and closing them up. It certainly must have seemed a useful effort to Le Corbusier and the

others, more than adequately justified by their sense of the oppressive shadows of the past and their faith in a future that would sweep the past away. By now, we have seen the past swept away often enough to speak with sense as well as sentiment when we demand to maintain our connections, or reinvest them. Then those of us—and that's most of the world by now—who lead lives complicatedly divorced from a single place in which we can find our roots, can have, through the channels of our mind and our memories, a built environment that helps reestablish those roots.

For Moore, an essential aspect of any future architecture is the cheerfully ironic application of known historic elements and of "things from everyday life." This addition of applied or painted ornaments or decorations differentiates itself from Venturi's intellectual irony and symbolism. For Moore, this is an attempt and a means to give back to "places" their own identity.

PRINCIPLE 1: + *Living in and speaking of places* + *(16, p. 68, and 17, p. 12).*

CHARLES MOORE

GENERAL PRINCIPLES

+ Buildings should be objects that speak for themselves. They should talk about their location, their construction, and about the people who made them and who use them + (16, p. 64, 17, p. 12).

+ Buildings are not merely a play of forms in light; at the same time, they are important as transmitters of memories, taking the things of everyday life as generally intelligible "metaphors" + (10, p. 302).

+ Consideration of the existing, that is, historical situation (preexisting "reality") + (16, p. 64).

JUSTIFICATION

+ "Order" and "reality" are essential elements of architecture. A "neutral" building cannot consider the needs of people or of a complex and significant environment + (16, p. 67).

+ Overcoming the distance between user and architecture—that is, the environment of the space + (16, p. 10).

Prevention of a possible isolation of the new structure from the user and from its surroundings (structure of the city or character of the landscape) (8, p. 124).

Buildings as objects that "speak for themselves and tell stories":

Residential Development, Church Street South
New Haven, CT
1969

Buildings as important transmitters of generally intelligible memories:

Kresge College
Santa Cruz, CA
1974

Consideration of preexisting or historical situations:

Sea Ranch Condominium No. 1
Sea Ranch, CA
1965

TOWN-PLANNING LEVEL

Differentiated design of spaces and places to create a "varied and significant environment." Different arrangement for each residential unit.

OBJECT LEVEL

Clear characterization of individual zones:

1. Boundary between public and private zone by means of a wall slab
2. Entrance zone
3. Living zone
4. Sleeping zone/boundary of roof.

ZONE LEVEL

Clear presentation of construction parts and principles:

- Face brick
- Plastered wall
- Entrance cube.

Creation of "angular connections between the masses of a building" to differentiate the individual parts of the space and to identify different spatial situations (8, p. 125).

The façade has multiple rhythms due to arcades in front of the actual body of the building, with different unit spacing for the openings and the solid parts of the wall.

The "dummy" arcade is clearly separated from the actual building, identified as an element "hung in front" (8, p. 125).

Adaptation of the articulation of the building masses to the existing structure of the landscape. (The silhouette of the body of the building follows the form of the landscape, use of local timber.)

Characterization of the form of the building as "an accidental part of a village," through various horizontal boundaries to the body of the building.

The characterization as a rural wooden building is an analogy to the well-known wooden barns, whose construction is clearly visible.

ARCHITECTURAL CHARACTERISTICS

TOWN-PLANNING LEVEL

OBJECT LEVEL

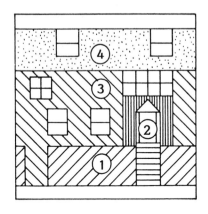

ZONE LEVEL

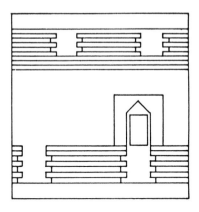

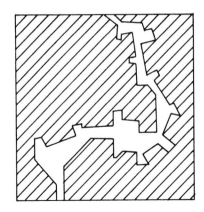

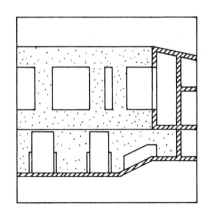

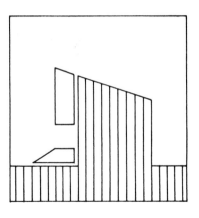

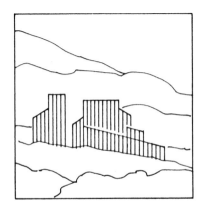

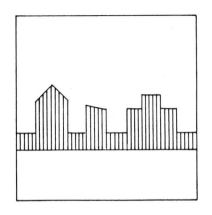

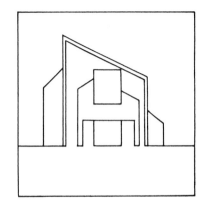

PRINCIPLE 2: + Freedom of speech for architecture + (16, p. 68).

CHARLES MOORE

GENERAL PRINCIPLES

Buildings must have freedom to "speak" and "narrate": "Buildings can tell us something . . . about how they were built and about the people who use them and who built them . . ." (10, p. 277).

+ A building should be as "descriptive" as possible: for example, it should tell us how it was built (material or construction) or how it was used (housing, parking station, or student residence) + (10, p. 277).

+ The overall layout of a building should express its own identity + (10, p. 277).

JUSTIFICATION

"If architecture is to survive in the human consciousness, then the things buildings can say, be they wistful or wise or powerful or gentle or heretical or silly, have to respond to the wide range of human feelings" (16, p. 68).

Only "narrative" architecture can be registered and stored in the human consciousness.

+ Applied ornament as the most important addition to the "beauty" of the building. +
+ Stimulation of the human senses to the perception of space, in contrast to the "pure" form of the "International Style" + (8, p. 282).

Freedom of buildings to "speak" and "narrate":

Kresge College
Santa Cruz, CA
1974

A building should be descriptive:

Kresge College
Santa Cruz, CA
1974

Expression of the building's own identity:

Kresge College
Santa Cruz, CA
1974

TOWN-PLANNING LEVEL

Arrangement of ''trivial monuments'' along a pedestrian space: arcaded walks, entrances, meeting points, etc.

OBJECT LEVEL

''Narrative'' façades are placed in front of important buildings, like stage scenery, to signify and emphasize special uses.

ZONE LEVEL

Differentiation between, and emphasis on, entrances, through a sequence of differentiated architectural elements. 1–3: Sequence of paths through a building.

A series of different buildings, whose shapes depend on their different use and significance:
1. Entrance; 2. Post office; 3. Telephone; 4. Laundry; 5. Speakers' corner; 6. Arch; 7. Café; 8. Meeting point.

Arrangement of arcades to signify a ''residential type,'' or arrangement of access galleries as elements of a semipublic zone.

Emphasis on the use and construction through the superimposition of a painted façade. Characterization of a specific place.

Constant change of direction and orientation of the individual elements.

Addition of ''decorative'' accessories to the actual body of the building—''stage-scenery ornament.''

Interrelationship of reality and illusion: openings and painted ''deceptions.''

TOWN-PLANNING LEVEL

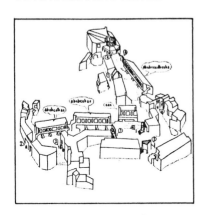

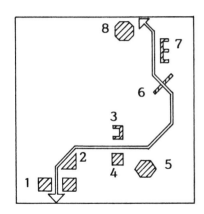

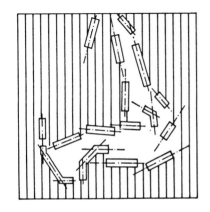

OBJECT LEVEL

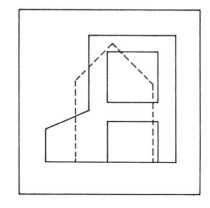

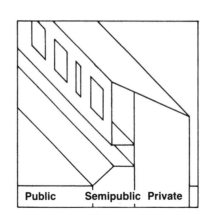

Public   Semipublic   Private

ZONE LEVEL

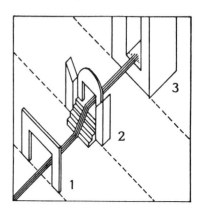

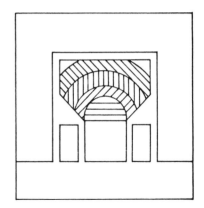

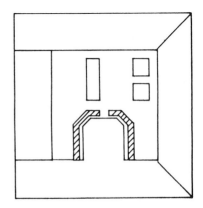

PRINCIPLE 3: + Buildings must be inhabitable + (16, p. 69).

CHARLES MOORE

GENERAL PRINCIPLES

"Buildings must be inhabitable for the body, the spirit, and the human memory. . . . The will to inhabit is one of the fundamental human needs" (16, p. 69).

+The architecture should express the fact that the user has at his disposal a small part of the world to inhabit and enhance + (17, p. 13).

+In design, the functions should be ordered, as in a puzzle, independently of "art or society." The standard of the architecture should be enhanced, at small expense, through symbols + (10, p. 302).

JUSTIFICATION

+A building should achieve what it has to achieve—with ordinary and simple means—for example, to define a personal and private living space + (10, p. 296).

Separation and distance between the interior and the exterior (private and public space) of a building.

The symbolic significance of the places that are being created is an advantage for the inhabitants and at the same time a reaction to the "almost hopeless condition" of the environment, designed with the normal architectural expedients + (10, p. 302).

Buildings must be inhabitable for the body, the spirit, and the human memory. (See the Residential Development, New Haven, below.)

Provision of a zone for personal design, and clear differentiation between public and private space:

Residential Development, Church Street South
New Haven, CT
1969

Enhancement of architecture through symbols:

Kresge College
Santa Cruz, CA
1974

Charles Moore   **97**

TOWN-PLANNING LEVEL	OBJECT LEVEL	ZONE LEVEL
	Clear separation of the public, semi-public and private zones.	Reduction of the planning problems to their essential aspects—for example, in the plan or in the number of window openings. ". . . I insist on more windows . . . but I am not interested in fighting over the skirting boards, the decoration, or the walls" (10, p. 276).
	Creation of diverse intermediate zones (buffer zones) between the public space of the street and the private residential zone: entrance courts, staircases.	Distance between the public street level and the private entrance/ residential level through clear transitions.
Articulation of space through symbols along a pedestrian space: "telephone arcade," "open-air theater," "speaker's corner."	Allocation of running water, or of a fountain, as a symbol of the utilization "laundry."	Emphasis on the location and the utilization "telephone" through the specific shaping of a "telephone arcade."

TOWN-PLANNING LEVEL **OBJECT LEVEL** **ZONE LEVEL**

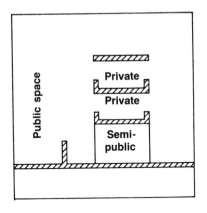 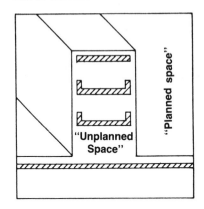

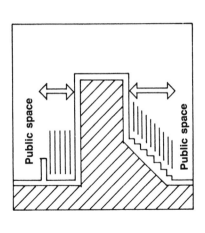 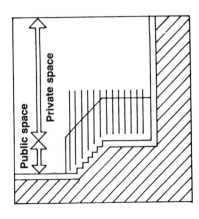

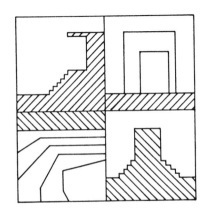 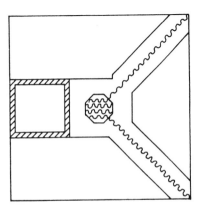 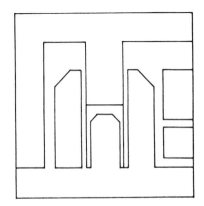

PRINCIPLE 4: + Memory of places + (17, p. 31).

CHARLES MOORE

GENERAL PRINCIPLES

Architecture needs a memory of "places." The human body must be able to perceive the significance of a place. The "place" should not merely be visible with the eyes but perceived by the brain + (17, p. 13).

JUSTIFICATION

+ The memory demands more than the comprehension of geometric conditions, such as right and left, or top and bottom, but also requires characteristic forms and content, for the senses and the visual perception + (16, p. 69).

+ Buildings should receive the designer's individual imprint + (10, p. 279).

One should be able to carry away a definite memory of the place in which one lives (10, p. 279).

+ Buildings should be connected to one another through a chain of events + (10, p. 279).

+ The path to a place should constitute a valued memory + (10, p. 279).

*Architecture needs a memory of
"places":*

*Kresge College
Santa Cruz, CA
1974*

*Buildings have their own individual
imprint:*

*Residential Development, Church
Street South
New Haven, CT
1969*

*Connection of buildings to one
another through a chain of events.
(See Residential Development, New
Haven, above.)*

TOWN-PLANNING LEVEL

Specific significance (function) is assigned to each public space (individual paths and squares).

OBJECT LEVEL

Different functions have a different significance for the memory:

A: Laundry "façade"
B: Telephone "façade"
C: Entrance "façade"
D: Post-office "façade"

ZONE LEVEL

Characterization of the "entrance." Definition of the boundaries of the different uses of space.

Differentiation in the creation of spaces through the different allocation of different groups of buildings to different public spaces (streets and squares).

Equal entrances to buildings receive their individual characters through variation in the colors used.

Supplementation of the body of the building by superimposed painted geometric patterns.

Public spaces (streets and squares) are differentiated by different "events"—for example, by the type of planting.

Creation of a sequence of differently arranged public spaces (streets and squares).

TOWN-PLANNING LEVEL

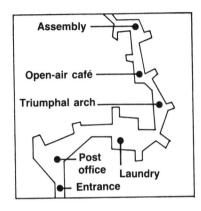

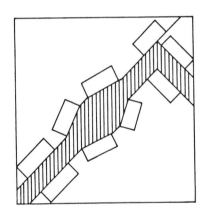

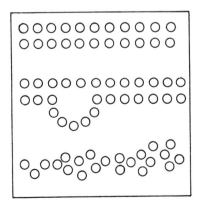

OBJECT LEVEL

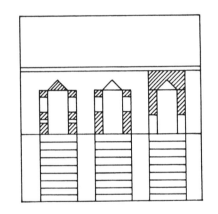

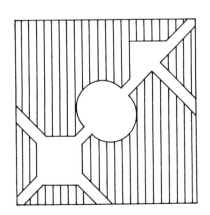

ZONE LEVEL

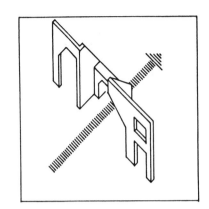

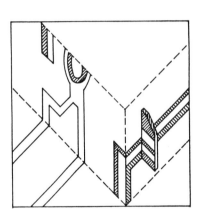

PRINCIPLE 5: + Perception of the interrelationship of space and time + (16, p. 69).

CHARLES MOORE

GENERAL PRINCIPLES

"The spaces which we perceive, the forms which we see, the way in which we move in our spatial environment, shall stimulate the human memory through its reconstruction of interrelations between space and time" (16, p. 69 and 17, pp. 13–14).

+"Constantly changing views" shall be made possible by creating a space with a "sequence of scenes" + (10, p. 281).

Creation of "urban spaces" (10, p. 279).

JUSTIFICATION

Avoidance of a uniform and monotonous sequence of spaces.

As a contrast to the oversized freeways.

Stimulation of the human memory through the reconstruction of the relationship between space and time:

Kresge College
Santa Cruz, CA
1974

Space creation as a series of scene sequences with changing views:

Residential Development, Church Street South
New Haven, CT
1969

Creation of urban spaces:

Residential Development, Church Street South
New Haven, CT
1969

TOWN-PLANNING LEVEL

"We would like to reestablish our contacts with tradition" (16, p. 69). Symbols and signs from "familiar" historical elements from the past. The octagon of Hadrian's Villa, the triumphal arch, the fountain of the Alhambra.

"Changing views" in the horizontal space of the streets through different spatial forms.

+ Spaces can be positive and memorable, if their landscape is correctly designed + (10, p. 279). Layout of the positive and negative features of the terrain with elements such as trees and surfaces of water.

OBJECT LEVEL

"Great, white surfaces" create an image of a Mediterranean village. (8, p. 125).

Vertical articulation of the street space through the differentiation of the edges or planes at the boundaries of the space.

Dimensions for the space of the streets and squares that are at a human scale—that is, they are on a small scale, and one can take them in at one glance.

ZONE LEVEL

Two-story public arcade as an element of Mediterranean architecture.

Interposed screens (like stage scenery) make it possible to characterize a particular place through "changing views" or a differentiated field of vision.

TOWN-PLANNING LEVEL

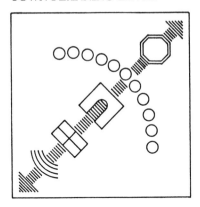

OBJECT LEVEL

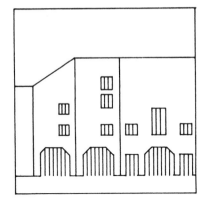

ZONE LEVEL

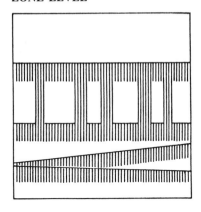

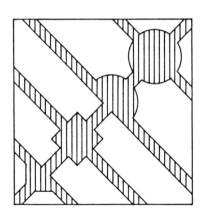

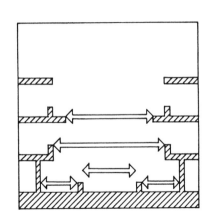

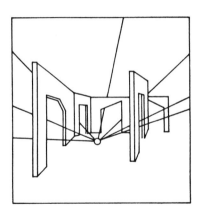

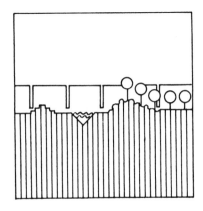

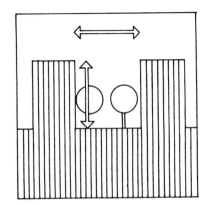

Charles Moore **107**

On the occasion of the XV Triennale in Milan in 1973, a publication entitled *Architettura Razionale* appeared; its author was Aldo Rossi. In subsequent years the goals formulated by Rossi in this publication for a "return to the original order in the language of form" in architecture (22, p. 416) and the demand for the employment of pure, rationally comprehensible symbols, such as the cube, the cone, and the pyramid, for the design of urban spaces, founded a new and today much-discussed architectural movement— Rationalism.

With the concept of Rationalism, Rossi returns to the Italian discussions on architecture that took place in the 1920s and 1930s. At that time a group of Rationalists demanded "the use of rational methods in architecture, the reduction of the multitude of forms to a few, basic types, and the renunciation of individually coined solutions" (4, p. 196). This movement considered itself a reaction to the dominant academic concept in Italy at that time.

Rossi sees the first historic statement for a Rationalist architecture in the revolutionary architecture of Boullée and Ledoux. The employment of simple, clear, basic, stereometric forms, which are the result of analogies to building forms from the early history of architecture, plays a central role in the work of Aldo Rossi. A decisive design factor is the search for familiar signs and symbols that are of significance to architecture because of their human associations. The recognition of architecture as a traditional symbol founded on history provides him with a logical structural system for architectural spaces. At the same time, Rossi always endeavors to find "basic types" for each particular use. Consequently, in his residential designs he alludes to "the basic types of habitation, which have been developed over long periods in the architecture of our cities" (15, p. 216).

It is Rossi's starting point that these archetypes of the home "have not altered from antiquity to the present day" (10, p. 28). In accordance with this analogy, "each corridor is a street, each courtyard a public square, and each building reproduces the localities of the city" (15, p. 216). These considerations are essentially the basis of the design of the apartment building Gallaratese in Milan.

In the theoretical and architectural work of Aldo Rossi, architectural forms are derived from the history of architecture. Rossi attempts, through a rational reference to history and tradition, to derive architectural elements that provide a new basis for design. Through this transformation of forms and types he stimulates a new or reawakened consciousness of architectural elements in the design of the environment. With this conception, Rossi opposes the functional trends which are a consequence of the Modern Movement. According to him, the functional interpretation of town-planning elements does not lead to a clarification or improvement of the housing situation; rather, it does more to hinder the analysis of form and consequently the possibility of an understanding of the true laws of architecture.

Aldo Rossi has so far had few opportunities to transform his comprehensive theories into real architecture. His visions are shown in a multiplicity of almost poetical images and drawings, from which one can imagine a possible reality. His exquisite drawings show all the ramifications that are possible in the transformation of form, and their significance. The coldness and almost monotonous transformation of his ideas in the realization of Gallaratese is therefore the more surprising. The visual appearance of this layout, and of a series of his projects, reminds one of the formal expression of the buildings of the Modern Movement. Reference to the historical tradition or familiarity with signs and symbols are barely noticeable and are almost displaced by an intrusive and dominant geometry.

GENERAL PRINCIPLES	JUSTIFICATION
Use of "basic housing types" as an "analogy" to the "architecture of the city" (15, p. 216).	"The building reproduces the locations of the city." + The basic types have been developed by the long process of architecture in the city, and they are consequently familiar places for habitation + (15, p. 216).
Employment of familiar "types" for residential buildings (16, p. 40).	". . . the types of the residential buildings have not altered from antiquity to the present day . . ." (16, p. 60). "Many ugly buildings cannot be classified as being of a particular type, nor can they be traced back to any particular cause" (9, p. 10).
"Reflection (use) on (strict) geometric form." Reduction to elementary, basic forms (9, p. 10).	". . . the use of geometric forms is a constant peculiarity of architecture" (9, p. 10).

Use of basic housing types:

Apartment Building Gallaratese
Milan, Italy
1970

Employment of "familiar" types for residential buildings:

Apartment Building Gallaratese
Milan, Italy
1970

Use of elementary, geometric, basic forms:

Apartment Building Gallaratese
Milan, Italy
1970

TOWN-PLANNING LEVEL

"The courtyard" between the buildings is "a public square" of the city (15, p. 216).

OBJECT LEVEL

The "corridor" or the "typological form of the access gallery . . . represents an inner, high-level street" (9, p. 10). It "represents a form of life steeped in the history of the people, in domestic intimacy and its associations" (15, p. 216).

ZONE LEVEL

Portico as an urban element in the street (11, p. 41).

". . . The type 'access gallery' is a form of life founded on the history of the people, founded on domestic intimacy . . ." (15, p. 216).

"The entire building unfolds itself along a horizontal thoroughfare ('street')" (9, p. 10).

Assembly of a general layout by the addition of clear and simple major forms.

Presentation of the building as a major geometric form, clear and simple.

Square/circle/quadrilateral or cube/cylinder/parallelepiped are decisive forms for constructional (columns, wall slabs) and functional (windows, floors) elements.

TOWN-PLANNING LEVEL

OBJECT LEVEL

ZONE LEVEL

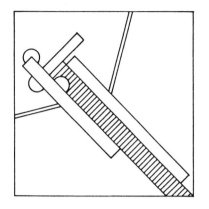

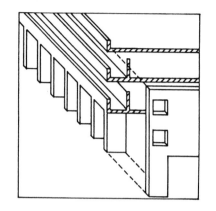

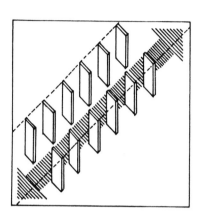

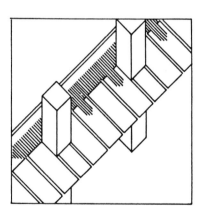

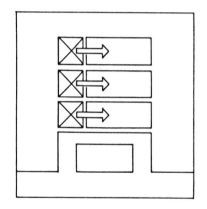

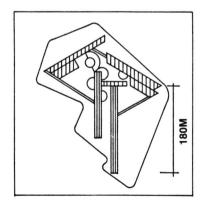

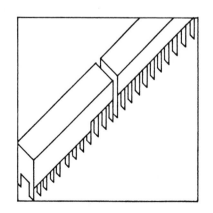

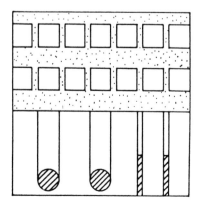

GENERAL PRINCIPLES

Characterization of ''technical'' and ''functional'' aspects (9, p. 10).

JUSTIFICATION

Technical aspects as determinants of form.

''. . . for a residential building we need (only) establish the structural things'' (11, p. 42).

''. . . the interior space of a dwelling changes in the course of time . . .'' (11, p. 42). ''The really progressive point of view of architecture consists of making life possible, not hindering it'' (17, p. 11).

Representation of the technical and/or functional aspects in the articulation of the body of the building:

Apartment Building Gallaratese Milan, Italy 1970

Avoidance of unalterable fixed points in the plan. Potential for alterations in the future, should the demand for residential accommodation change (See Gallaratese, above).

TOWN-PLANNING LEVEL

Articulation of the mass of the building by technical necessities (for example, an expansion joint). Clear emphasis through an oversized "joint" and by giving prominence to this notable "place" through special columns or a special entrance.

OBJECT LEVEL

Presentation of the expansion joint as the "formally most important place" in the plan. Arrangement of special elements, such as stairs and oversized columns.

"Every tenant can choose the design (and also the size) of his apartment himself" (11, p. 43).

ZONE LEVEL

The zone where the access gallery opens out vertically is shown both outside and inside by a special design of the window openings:

- Large openings
- Diagonals
- Metal grates

"The architect should provide surroundings that solve certain defined problems, but interfere as little as possible with one's private life" (17, p. 11). Choice of:

- 2-room type
- 4-room type
- 4½-room type.

TOWN-PLANNING LEVEL

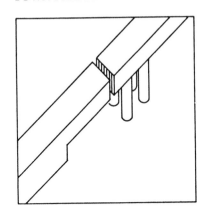

OBJECT LEVEL

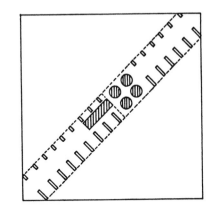

ZONE LEVEL

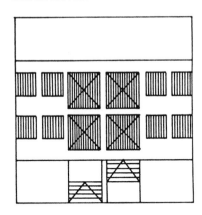

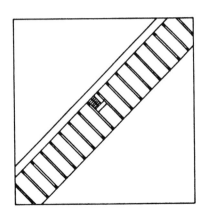

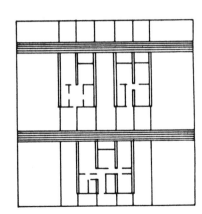

Oswald Matthias Ungers

The young German architect Oswald Matthias Ungers first participated in the international architectural discussion on the problems of contemporary architecture at the CIAM Conference at Aix-en-Provence in 1954. At Aix-en-Provence he began to criticize Le Corbusier's *Five Points for a New Architecture*. As far as he was concerned, the arguments formulated therein took too little account of the historical development of architecture; according to Ungers, these concepts followed purely functional trends.

This opinion on the significance of the Modern Movement, expressed as early as the middle 1950s, is the essential hallmark to this day of the theoretical and realized work by Ungers. During the last decade his activity has been essentially reduced to the search for new forms and for a vocabulary for the renewal of architectural thinking. Ungers began twenty years ago, in a multitude of projects and essays and as part of his teaching activity, to lay down the guidelines of a new architectural conception. On the whole, his work tends to lean toward Rationalism, although

Ungers has never unequivocally associated himself with that movement. This classification is based essentially on the visual appearance of his architectural projects; on the other hand, his theoretical principles differ quite appreciably from those of this movement. The architectural elements used by Ungers can be found among representatives of the Rationalist idea, as for example the brothers Krier, Aldo Rossi, and James Stirling. Starting with the meaning of the design process and the problems as well as the meaning of architecture, Ungers has developed a series of presentations that have decisively influenced discussions of contemporary architecture.

As the leitmotiv of his thinking about design with the aid of conceptual images, metaphors, and analogies (8, pp. 1,650 *et seq*.), Ungers distinguishes between two possible modes: empirical thinking and imaginative-morphological thinking. According to Ungers, the imaginative-morphological way of thinking is correct and necessary for architectural design. This mode of thinking does not search for the reality of

individual elements or of an object from the subjective point of view but looks for a universal statement and meaning based on experience. These experiences refer to the familiar outward forms of architecture, with special reference to the historical experiences of users who have made observations on the perception of individual buildings. As "general content" and "comprehensive concept," this universal idea establishes an inner coherence among all the individual elements, and for Ungers it is the most important characteristic of the design. In conjunction with the demand for historical architectural evidence, it is not accidental that the imaginative-morphological mode of thought already played a special part in the philosophical literature of "morphological idealism," of humanism, and of the Renaissance. At the center of this mode of thinking lies the correlation between the perception of an architectural form, thinking as an intellectual order, and the development of images, and following from that the intrinsic recognition of the special properties of an (architectonic) object. According to Ungers, it is only through this correlation with perception that man is enabled to create a reality and to structure this through conceptual images.

In accordance with this mode of thought, Ungers formulated seven "Theses for Design as a Morphological Process" (9, p. 97):

1. Design is based on the logical analysis of real situations; for example, the structure of an existing city. "The design is developed in accordance with the character of the place of which it is to become a part" (9, p. 97). In this connection, Ungers always points to the "genius loci" of the problem whose realization is under discussion.

2. Design has two levels of reality—one is planned, the other is unplanned, accidental. On the first level, it receives a general interpretation. On the second level, a special solution is produced by reference to architectural models and rules.

3. Design is a permanent stress field, full of suspense, in which individual steps constantly uncover new alternatives.

4. Design should emphasize the urban character of architecture; that is, architecture should, within the framework of its environment, accept a "uniting and mediating" role.

5. "Design with images, metaphors, and analogies . . . the design process from materialistic problem-solving to a richer, more imaginative, and visionary working process" (9, p. 97).

6. Design is a morphological process (a transformation of the apparent form) that translates physical into conceptual reality; it is an attempt to find ideas in visual form.

7. Design is a creative process for the conception of a minimal solution with a maximum of possible interpretations, taking into account the perception of the user.

In addition to the mode of thought developed in the design process for the solution of problems, Ungers considers a meaningful discussion using the new architectural concepts as being of decisive importance. He talks of a "humanist architecture" and thus attaches himself consciously to the architectural concepts of the Age of Reason in the eighteenth and nineteenth centuries. He sees in this conception of architecture a deliberate contrast to the "antihistoric trends" of the dogmas and manifestos of the Modern Movement.

The "humanist architecture" is derived from the consciousness of historical continuity, and it does not aim to transform people. This conception reminds one of the ideas of Schinkel, based on

historical continuity, or Le Corbusier's analysis of Antiquity and of Ottoman Turkey. Thus, Ungers also believes "that the most valuable lesson to be drawn from Schinkel's endeavors is the ability to absorb the environment, the existing buildings and spaces into one's own architecture" (10, p. 15). The most important criterion of the so-called humanist architecture, according to Ungers, is the discussion of an environment that develops naturally and bears the stamp of its time. Of decisive importance for the realization of this architecture, apart from a formal consciousness, is the historical and cultural consciousness of the architect to bear the responsibility for the design of his environment.

With the demands of a "humanist architecture" Ungers couples the design of conceptual images, as opposed to designing a vague environment behind the veil of a functional or rational mystique. He is concerned with the design of a building, not with the fulfillment of a program, and with the expression of architectural spaces, not with the organization of functional sequences. An essential element of Ungar's design philosophy is the illustration of the formal interrelations in terms of the dimensions of the spaces, in contrast to a reduction of the problem to a system of a functional built environment.

GENERAL PRINCIPLES	JUSTIFICATION
+Creation of complexity in an urban order + (5, p. 15) +Illustration of a "morphology"; that is, variations on a basic plan. +	+Break with the dogmas of Mies van der Rohe and Gropius with regard to the goal of "the greatest possible simplification" in the layout of a building complex + (5, p. 15).
". . . multiplicity of different buildings and spatial characters" (5, p. 15).	+Humanist demand for multiplicity, like that of Alberti, the Renaissance theoretician + (5, p. 15).
+Creation of a relationship between the sequences of buildings and spaces that is full of suspense + (5, p. 16).	For the genesis and perception of spaces that provide orientation and direction (5, p. 16).

Creation of complexity through the image of basic forms in a morphology:

Student Residence Twente, Germany Competition, 1964

Creation of a multiplicity of spatial forms and characteristics (see Student Residence, above).

Creation of a relationship between the sequences of buildings and spaces that is full of suspense (see Student Residence, above).

TOWN-PLANNING LEVEL

Creation of complexity through the arrangement of different building complexes with a multiplicity of forms. Superimposition on the plan of modified geometric patterns, taking account of the symmetry and the axes.

OBJECT LEVEL

Multiple offerings for the arrangement of the individual rooms into groups, for example:

- Straight rows
- Clusters
- Creation of courtyards
- Arrangement in stepped or straight lines

ZONE LEVEL

+The formal multiplicity is matched by a user multiplicity: single rooms, apartments, or groups of apartments for communal living in units of two or three, in different neighborhood arrangements and in different spatial forms.

Allocation of different groups of rooms to different external spaces:

- Living on a courtyard
- Living along a street
- Living along a lane
- Living on a square
- Living on a slope.

Composition of the total layout of the plan from clearly defined geometric units, which are, however, different.

The starting point is geometry, the plan shapes thus derived, and their individual transformations. Composition elements:

- square/cube
- circle/sphere
- semicircle/hemisphere
- half cylinder
- quadrilateral/parallelepiped, etc.

Creation of spaces that provide orientation and direction. "The lane widens progressively, and passes into an open square without, however, conveying the impression that the buildings which form its boundaries are merely discourteously standing around" (5, p. 16).

+A student village is not a settlement of multiple units arranged in rows but a miniature "town." Addition of differentiated units made appropriately different + (5, p. 16).

An architecturally designed group of trees, planted to show that green need not be understood as landscape green. ". . . A square of trees is a sign that declares the intention that even nature must become a part of the geometric context" (5, p. 16).

TOWN-PLANNING LEVEL

OBJECT LEVEL

ZONE LEVEL

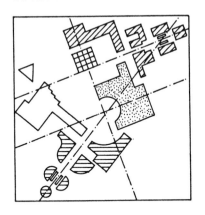
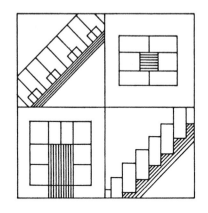
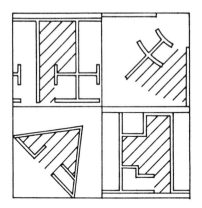

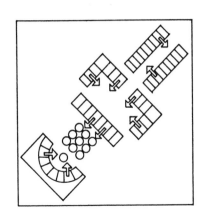

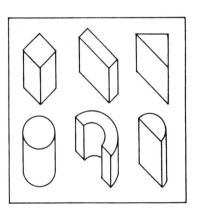

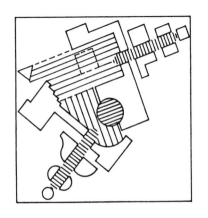

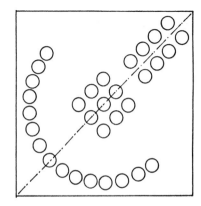

GENERAL PRINCIPLES	JUSTIFICATION
"Creation of urban space." "A design shall emphasize the urban character of the architecture, not its properties as an object standing on its own" (3, p. 270, 9, p. 97).	Creation of space from a landscape. "Architecture is living space and environment, and it can consequently absorb urban functions and incorporate them . . ." (9, p. 97).
A series of "artificial" squares (plazas) shall be offered as an urban space adventure, for the "adventurous experience" of an "urban space (3, p. 272)."	"Architecture cannot claim any 'absolute' values, but is relativized through a permanent confrontation and an analytical discussion with the real factors" (10, p. 135).
"Unequivocal formulation of the outdoor spaces—in the sense of an architectural harmony" (3, p. 272).	The impression conveyed should be one that has consciously been conceived in terms of space. "The user should . . . be consciously stimulated to appreciate that he is not just anywhere, but in a quite special space . . ." (3, p. 273).

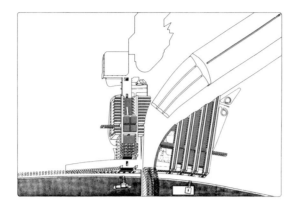

Creation of an urban space that appears urban:

Wallraf-Richartz Museum Competition Cologne, Germany 1965

Urban space adventure created by "artificial" squares (plazas) (see Wallraf-Richartz Museum, above).

Unequivocal formulation of the outdoor spaces (see Wallraf-Richartz Museum, above).

TOWN-PLANNING LEVEL	OBJECT LEVEL	ZONE LEVEL
Creation of a circumscribed and comprehensible volume as an "urban space."	Use of clearly readable and unequivocally formulated masses, which surround the various zones of the space.	
A series of squares (plazas) that are designed to appear different and are put to different use.	Clear and geometric design of the individual spaces for the squares and streets; horizontal boundaries, for example, by geometrically arranged rows of trees; vertical boundaries by well-balanced "squares."	Development of the public squares and streets as "sculpture gardens." Creation of an "artistic" design for the squares by the use of rows of trees, geometric patterns for the pavement, and sculptures.
Clear and unequivocal sequence of outdoor spaces.	The lines bounding the space (the edges and corners of the building masses) mold the design; they are clearly readable and comprehensible.	Architectural treatment of the planting. Trees as spheres, cubes, or pyramids.

TOWN-PLANNING LEVEL **OBJECT LEVEL** **ZONE LEVEL**

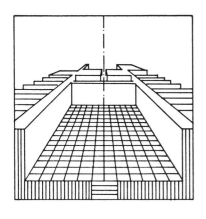
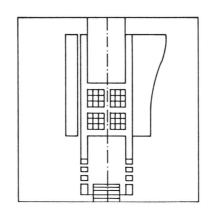

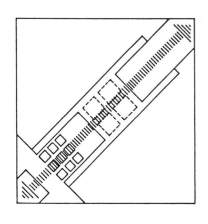
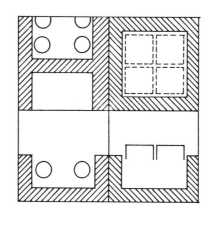
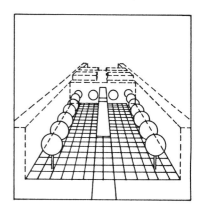

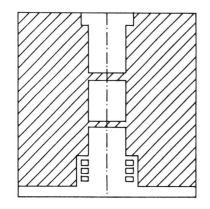
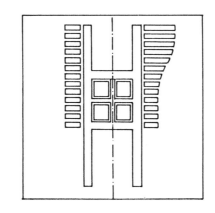
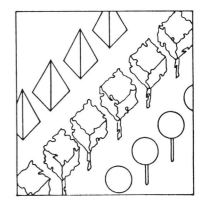

GENERAL PRINCIPLES

Emphasis on the "capacity for spatial experience"—support for different qualities of experience (3, p. 273).

+ The building (museum) should be an object in which it is possible to walk and see things, an object of the city, a space of the city + (3, p. 274).

Creation of a special spatial element—introduction of narrative moments.

JUSTIFICATION

Raised consciousness of being present in an artistic (urbane) space, in contrast to a space that has no extreme qualities, and in which a spatial experience is inconceivable (3, p. 273).

+ The museum shall be a part of a municipal communication network or circulation system. Without entering the building called "museum," the nonvisitors shall be able to participate in the "museum" experience + (3, p. 273).

Creation of an unmistakable identity for the individual spaces.

Emphasis on a capacity for spatial experience (see Wallraf-Richartz Museum, pictured earlier).

The building as an object in which it is possible to walk (see Wallraf-Richartz Museum, pictured earlier).

Introduction of narrative moments (see Wallraf-Richartz Museum, pictured earlier).

Oswald Matthias Ungers   **129**

TOWN-PLANNING LEVEL	OBJECT LEVEL	ZONE LEVEL
Different treatment of form and material for the spaces of the individual streets and squares.	Homogeneous and impressive design for the entrance—for example, rose-colored marble.	
Public paths "within" the museum—that is, through the buildings.	The articulation of space results from the "public" paths. One experiences the space, as well as the uses to which it is put and its functions, without having to enter the building.	
	Design of the entrance as "a picture by de Chirico, translated into space" (4, p. 28).	Introduction of surprise effects to create a special event. Multiplicity (in this case quadruplication) of an equestrian statue as monument.

TOWN-PLANNING LEVEL **OBJECT LEVEL** **ZONE LEVEL**

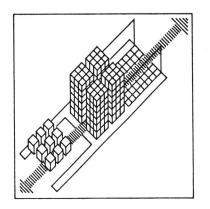 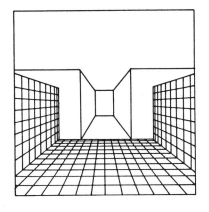

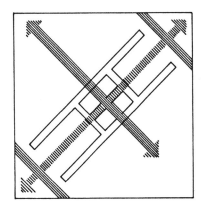 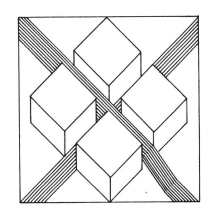

 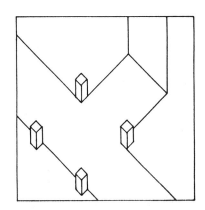

Oswald Matthias Ungers   **131**

In 1966 Venturi's book *Complexity and Contradiction in Architecture* appeared (23); a few years later a study of the Las Vegas Strip, *Learning from Las Vegas*, was published (24). These two publications started an international discussion on the condition of architecture at the end of the twentieth century. The Modern Movement, with all its modifications, had been accepted throughout the world as the recognized "style" of contemporary architecture until Venturi proclaimed his unusual attitude and formulated in detail his thoughts on the reshaping of the environment. Sociologists, psychologists, and other advocates of a comprehensive participation by the user in the planning (design) process had indeed, since the beginning of the 1960s, complained in increasing measure about the mistakes of modern architecture without, however, being able to point to possible remedies or appropriate action to obviate the "inhospitableness of our cities" (Mitscherlich). In this fast-stagnating phase of the pluralism of styles, Venturi and his team (Denise Scott Brown, Steven Izenour, John Rauch, and others) turned against the widely accepted semiofficial architecture and searched for a path to a better future.

Venturi studied the trivial commercial architecture of the Strip and the everyday world of the American suburb. For him, the study of this commercial "everyday" aesthetic was as important as the analysis of medieval Tuscan hill towns. His analyses attempted to safeguard the traces and remainders of picturesqueness and symbolism in the "ruined face of everyday" in the American everyday aesthetic with formal and iconographic inquiries (17, p. 843). In this process he searched for the elements of a picturesqueness, which he no longer saw realized in the "modern" environment. Venturi showed that the recognition of trite and trivial everyday architecture offered a possibility to overcome the inarticulateness of modern architecture. The analyses showed that the "common and ugly" world of everyday was described by a generally intelligible and universally valid language, which had thereby become a familiar part of everyone's environment. This architecture of everyday provided Venturi with a reservoir of formal stimulations and picturesque citations. In this connection Venturi coined the famous phrase: "Main Street is almost all right." The emphasis lies on "almost"; that is, the main street and its signs and symbols are "almost all right," and they could show us a possible way toward a "significant" architecture: "The Strip has shown us the symbolic content of architecture, and the possibility of an architectonic symbolic language" (9, p. 258). Venturi missed these signs and symbols among modern architects, because for them the building was purely "the result of structure, space and program" (9, p. 254). From this recognition, Venturi attempted to create an "impure" architecture. Sculptural, graphic, and other values should influence architecture by association; these are elements that existed previously during the era of Eclecticism and in almost every architectural movement. The building was reduced to a simple, protecting shell, and the significance of the building and its artistic expression could be treated separately. "This is antiarchitecture, and it defines architecture . . . as the decoration of construction" (9, p. 257). According to Venturi, this had shown itself earlier in the façades of the Gothic cathedral and the Italian palazzo. The history of architecture shows that architecture always concerned itself with iconographic and symbolic significance. According to this thesis, a Gothic cathedral is, for Venturi, a "decorated shed." According to Venturi's analysis, there is a contrast between the architecture of the building and the façade, which is quite separate from the architectonic space. "This advertisement functions better in front, the architecture better in the back" (9, p. 256). For Venturi, analogous to this recognition, "architectural symbols and explicit allusions are vital and unavoidable for the architect, as well as for the observer" (9, p. 262).

In his analyses of complexity and contradiction in architectural forms, Venturi referred to the historical Mannerism of the sixteenth century. Using a multitude of examples, he attempted to demonstrate the principles of form of an architecture that accepts "as well as": compromises, distortions, and multiplicity. In this process he derived the axiom that a system or principle must form the basic order of a design, but that this principle of order may subsequently be breached. Thus, in the residential building at Chestnut Hill, the symmetry of the body of the building is canceled out by the entrance zone, which is located off center; oversized openings form monumental elements that contrast with the actual dimensions of the body of the building; and the frontage—to separate the exterior from the interior— appears as a façade placed in front of the building, which has no relation to the design of the interior spaces of the building.

For Venturi, the reality of architecture is contradictory, complex, and nonhomogeneous. He consequently demands the recognition of multiplicity, indeed confusion, whether interior or exterior, accidental or planned, at all levels of experience (23). Only this contradiction, and the creation of a new world of art from the trite world of everyday, embodies for him a perceptible and therefore human architecture.

Recent discussions have evidently split the defenders and the opponents of Venturi's intentions into two opposed camps. The opponents see in these visions a total design of the environment with trivial "kitsch," neon lights, and Disneyland architecture, while the advocates of symbols and signs in architecture interpret it merely as a total irony. A cross section of this spectrum was presented at the First Architecture Biennale in Venice in 1980. One group apparently treated this show very earnestly, but its contributions could only be taken seriously in parts. It appears, and it is regrettable in these discussions, that they forgot about Venturi's real thesis or interpreted it too onesidedly; namely, the discussion of "whether . . . or." It is possible that much of Venturi's analysis and theory has been forgotten or has come into question in view of the buildings he has in fact realized. Theories must be modified, as Venturi himself says, or framed only after realization of the buildings. However, one should bear in mind the attempt to find elements and forms that enable the user to have more confidence in and access to the architectural environment, within the meaning of an architectural language. In this context, the experience of the historical development of architecture and of human needs play a particular role. The buildings of Venturi and his team contain a "most remarkable, ambiguous, and multi-layered blend of functionalism, pop, and Palladio" (17, p. 843), while at the same time the design of the actual body of the building is determined by a clear geometry or well-chosen proportions. These aspects of the architectonic design process are basically derived from the principles of classical design or from the inspiration of Le Corbusier or Louis Kahn, and they are also obvious design principles in Venturi's work.

GENERAL PRINCIPLES	**JUSTIFICATION**
''To emphasize the vestigial role of the street façade'' (23, p. 114).	''The urban character of the street suggested a building that would not be an independent pavilion, but instead would recognize the spatial demands of the street in front'' (23, p. 114).
+ Creation of signs and symbols + (9, p. 255). The impact of architecture should not proceed from the architecture itself + (9, p. 256).	''The history of architecture teaches us that architecture always concerned itself with iconographic and symbolic significance'' (9, p. 256).
Everyday things should be the model for the design of the body of the building—that is, existing and familiar conditions and characteristics (the character of the city and of the surrounding buildings) should be considered (9, p. 253).	A reminder of the known and familiar. ''Main Street is almost all right'' (9, p. 254).

Emphasis on the street frontage:

Guild House
Philadelphia, PA
1960–63

Creation of signs and symbols:

Guild House
Philadelphia, PA
1960–63

Everyday life as a model:

Guild House
Philadelphia, PA
1960–63

Robert Venturi   **135**

ARCHITECTURAL CHARACTERISTICS

TOWN-PLANNING LEVEL

". . . but instead should recognize the spatial demands of the street in front" (23, p. 114). Clear differentiation between front façade and back.

OBJECT LEVEL

Clear differentiation between front façade and back through different design of the lines or planes limiting the space.

ZONE LEVEL

+ Façade placed in front of the building to emphasize the front façade. It is separated from the actual body of the building to emphasize its character as a "deceptive dress." Emphasis on the symmetrical arrangement of a communal antenna through slots +.

Symbol for the scale of the motorist: oversized writing on the façade.

Tripartite division of the façade to increase the scale: The zone of the ground floor built with white glazed bricks;

- The normal stories
- A large arch to increase the scale and emphasize the roof zone.

Emphasis on the entrance zone through the arrangement of a symmetrical axis, and emphasis on this axis through an oversized column. The black granite of this column contrasts with the white brick front and emphasizes it.

The existing buildings form the prototype for the mass of the building to be added: equal form for the body of the building, simple geometry, similar and familiar dimensions for the body of the building in the space of the street—in contrast to the oversized façade.

Design of the side and back frontages in accordance with existing design principles:

- a façade with simple holes;
- dark brown brick walls

(Memories of historic block buildings and of the backs of multifamily houses in the "Edwardian style.")

As a symbol of a familiar façade, the well-known double-hung window is used in conjunction with brickwork. Emphasis on the axial arrangement of the window elements. Visible television antenna as a sign of habitation.

TOWN-PLANNING LEVEL

OBJECT LEVEL

ZONE LEVEL

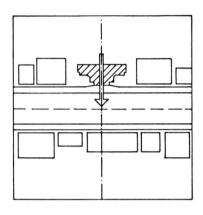
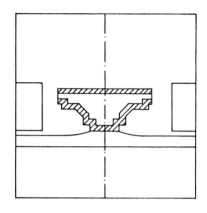
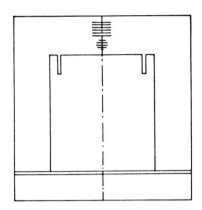

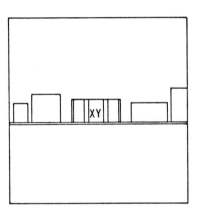
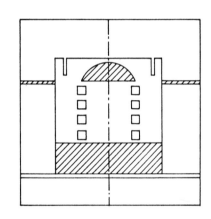
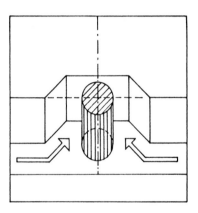

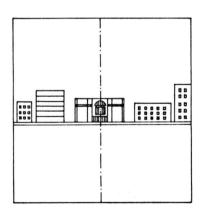
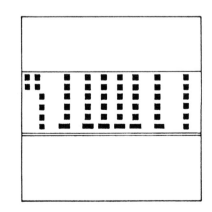
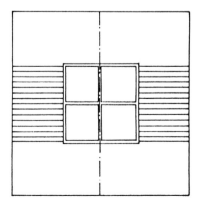

GENERAL PRINCIPLES

Separation of façade and the building behind it (9, p. 256). "Presentation of the decorated shed."

"Architectural elements should stand in contradiction to one another" (9, p. 256).

Creation of "impure architecture" (9, p. 257).
"Separation of significance and artistic expressions" from the actual building—that is, separation of building and decoration.

JUSTIFICATION

Emphasis on the main façade, because it contains the entrance. Differentiation "between the ceremonial entrance front and the ordinary back of the building" (14, p. 87).

+The history of architecture shows that the picture of a building has not always been "the harmonic result of construction, space and program" (for example, the façade of Amiens Cathedral) + (9, p. 256).

"Architecture is a building with applied decoration". "Decorated shed" (analogy to the façade of a Gothic cathedral) (26, p. 20).

Separation of the façade from the body of the building:

*Guild House
Philadelphia, PA
1960–63*

Contrast between the individual architectural elements:

*Residence
Chestnut Hill, PA
1962*

Creation of an "impure architecture"—that is, supplementation of the building with decoration:

*Franklin Court
Philadelphia, PA
1976*

TOWN-PLANNING LEVEL

Concentration of the street façade on a particular element—the symmetrical entrance—while the actual building recedes into the background.

OBJECT LEVEL

A "gigantic order" as a contrast to the six-story scale of the rest of the building:

- Entrance
- Articulation of the cornice at the roof level, in contrast to the small-scale articulation of the intermediate stories

ZONE LEVEL

Increase in scale through the introduction of a symmetrical gigantic order, which emphasizes the main façade ("monumentality of the street façade"). Superimposition of the articulation of the intermediate stories on a smaller scale.

"The inside spaces, as represented in plan and section, are complex and distorted in their shapes and interrelationships. On the other hand, the outside form—as represented by the parapeted wall and the gable roof, which enclose the complexities and distortions—is simple and consistent" (23, p. 117).

The gable sides, "placed in front," appear from the eaves side as parapeted walls. Clear representation of the contradictions through the visible edges of the wall slabs. A supposedly "simple" and "uniform" impression of the body of the building is canceled.

Clear accentuation of the decoration. The decoration is the essential element; the actual building recedes into the background, or it is entirely placed underground—"mock architecture."

Associative influence on architecture of the values of sculpture, graphics, painting, and other art forms (9, p. 250). Symmetrical park layout of the eighteenth century, in which symmetry appears only partly in the structure of the plan.

Creation of the atmosphere of the eighteenth century through cited elements of decoration. In that process, the type of restoration appropriate for monuments is consciously avoided:

- Fanlight/Fence
- Pergola/Trellis

TOWN-PLANNING LEVEL

OBJECT LEVEL

ZONE LEVEL

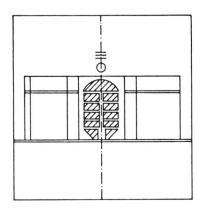

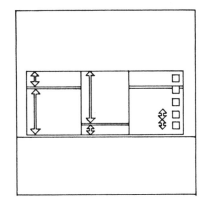

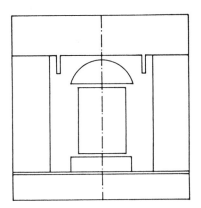

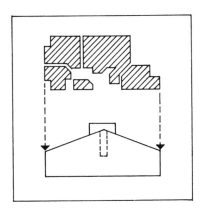

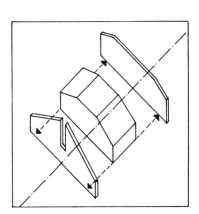

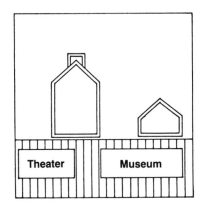

Theater

Museum

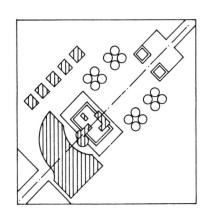

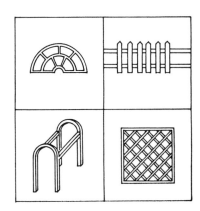

GENERAL PRINCIPLES

The illustration of "complexities" and "contradictions" ". . . at the same time complex and simple, open and closed, large and small . . ." (14, p. 99).

JUSTIFICATION

Orthodox modern architecture neglects the motive for interpreting different requirements, which deserve equal consideration (23).

.

"Complexity (multiplicity) and contradiction . . ." (23).

". . . as opposed to simplification and flight into the picturesque" (23).

+ Consideration for the existing or original landscape or city structure + (9, p. 253, 18, p. 59).

+ The existing buildings may be good; this contrasts with the concept that "everything that is already there is totally wrong" + (9, p. 253).
+ Illustration of and support for the existing or the original spaces + (18, p. 60).

Illustration of "complexity" and "contradiction":

Residence
Chestnut Hill, PA
1962

Against simplification and "flight into the picturesque":

Residence
Chestnut Hill, PA
1962

Consideration (by adaptation or continuation) of the existing conditions:

Franklin Court
Philadelphia, PA
1976

TOWN-PLANNING LEVEL

"The house is large and small at the same time"—that is, the individual dimensions are relatively small, while oversized signs are superimposed on its simple silhouette: elements that increase scale, symmetry (14, p. 99).

OBJECT LEVEL

Contradiction to the symmetry of the body of the building: openings in walls are unsymmetrically arranged, the entrance deviates in plan from the symmetrical axis (23).

The simple and clear form of the body of the building is placed on a different plan. "The abstract composition of this building almost equally combines rectangular, diagonal, and curving elements" (23, p. 121).

Adoption and continuation of existing and familiar formation of courtyards within the district. + Impression of historic courtyard construction + (9, p. 253).

ZONE LEVEL

"The dado increases the scale of the building all around because it is higher than you expect it to be. These moldings affect the scale in another way also: they make the stucco walls even more abstract, and the scale, usually implied by the nature of the materials, more ambiguous or noncommittal" (23, p. 120).

"The curves relate to the directional-spatial needs at the entry and outside stair; the spatial-expressive needs in section in the dining-room ceiling, which is contradictory to the outside slope of the roof" (23, p. 121).

Skeleton of a connecting element between two courtyards as a statement and an interpretation of a spatial contraction.

TOWN-PLANNING LEVEL

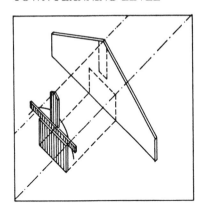

OBJECT LEVEL

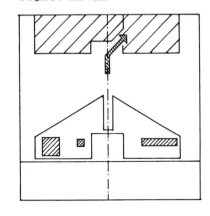

ZONE LEVEL

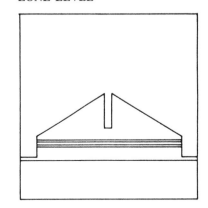

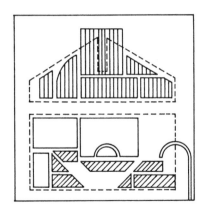

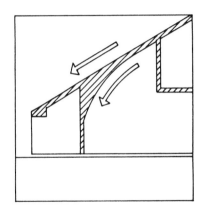

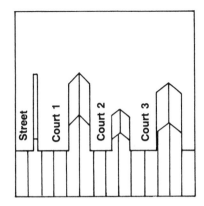

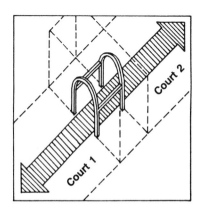

Design Principles and Architectural Characteristics

Comparison and Contrast of Principles and Characteristics

On the preceding pages a series of different architectural characteristics and their realizations were illustrated, together with analyses of general principles. By reference to selected buildings and projects, they offer a choice of actual concepts, ideas, and models for the architecture of the present and the future. For clarification, several of these architectural characteristics are considered on the following pages in the form of universal statements on the design activity of the architect.

As already mentioned, architectural characteristics can be formulated in words, in drawings, and in three-dimensional models to illustrate the real situation.

The realization of the built environment in terms of actual building materials is almost invariably based on design sketches and drawings in two dimensions and/or a model. Each of these sketches and drawings contains a multitude of decisions and principles. The following pages therefore present in graphic form a series of design elements and "architectural characteristics" for use in future work. This schematic presentation of design elements is intended to offer a choice of possible solutions in the form of sketches, which are the "language" of the designing architect. In this process an attempt is made to illustrate problems of space, geometry, design, layout, and coordination, as well as the solution of sociological and psychological problems by architectural means. The design elements show the smallest actual unit in the "synthesis" of a design concept. They are independent of use, building, or architect and are chosen for their individual architectural characteristics.

The architectural characteristics and the corresponding design elements are subjective; they form a small selection from a multitude too numerous to be included in this book. The design elements can help designers in the development of their own design concepts. However, to avoid ill-considered adaptations and incorrect interpretations of the movements and trends of any particular architectural epoch, it is of critical importance to be conscious of the interrelationships of the goals, formulated in words, and their translation into design and eventually into construction.

According to Joedicke (1), the characteristics can be classified in various ways—qualitative, quantitative, discrete, and so on. After limiting the analysis to the characteristics of a few architectural movements of the last decade, it can be seen that almost all the essential formulations of goals and principles are qualitative in nature. Quantitative aspects have only a small effect within the range of new and/or controversial design concepts for a new architecture. Moreover, it has been shown that qualitative characteristics can essentially be classified into three types:

- "rational" characteristics
- "symbolic" characteristics
- "psychological" characteristics

This division is the natural result of the corresponding formulation of principles, which aim to achieve "rational," "symbolic," or "psychological" goals. Surprisingly, this tripartite division is in accord with one proposed in 1938 by Fritz Schumacher for the design of buildings: "Effects due to reason, perception, and soul" (2). The individual characteristics are, in accordance with this division, allocated to three different categories of principles.

Rational Principles

Rational principles essentially describe "functions that have a rational objective" (3)—for example, a geometric layout and the coordination of units within the articulation of the mass of the building; the dimensioning of elements in accordance with the human scale; or the interrelationship of the function of the building and the choice between various structural systems. The principles allocated to this category are those whose realization is possible with design elements that can be essentially described as rational, or following a certain logic: the articulation of the fabric of the building, the manner of the allocation of spaces, the geometric organization of surfaces and spaces, the structural systems, the proportions of the dimensions of the spaces, etc. The "rational" principles do not, on the whole, deal with essentially new aspects. Schumacher sees in this category a close connection between function and construction.

Symbolic Principles

The group of symbolic principles contains a series of aspects that dominate the present discussion of Postmodern architecture. Schumacher talks about this range as transmitting an "artistic" truth, a "perceptual force." Contemporary trends show that

this range of architectural discussion, in particular, needs more attention and that the critics of the Modern Movement particularly deplore, in this range, the lack of use of the evidence of the past. "Proportions, rhythm, dimensions, ornament, color" (4), illumination, and connections between spaces and materials are characteristics that, with a renewed consciousness of their historical development, are again receiving special attention.

Psychological Principles

The realization and combination of rational and symbolic principles logically leads to a consideration of the psychological effects. To clarify this special group of principles, one can regard psychological aspects as the result of the social demands made on architecture. For example, in the 1960s there was a particular emphasis on the problems of user participation in the process of planning and design. Spaces created in accordance with these considerations, as, for example, the location of public footpaths within a building, were expected to promote social contacts. A series of principles was enunciated, which gave the user the opportunity to take part at the initial stages in the design of the building, to create leisure space for personal creativity and stimulation for personal fantasies.

The boundaries of the individual kinds of principles are fluid, and they allow for mutual influence. An analysis of individual designs has shown that in the period from 1945 to 1960, architecture was frequently influenced by rational considerations, and that only in the immediate past have symbolic and/or psychological aspects been given special consideration. The analysis has further shown that formulated principles were not of equal significance at all the planning levels. Accordingly, the column headed "Planning Levels and Principles" gives for each individual principle the particular planning levels that received special attention or that were frequently mentioned.

A—RATIONAL PRINCIPLES

ARCHITECTURAL CHARACTERISTICS

Creation of a flexible and adaptive building form for changes in use and function. Human scale through the use of comprehensible units.

Aggregation of equal or similar geometric units.
Combination of constant (cells) and flexible (bounded by columns) space elements.

Creation of a great "formal richness." Supplementation of the architecture with "ornamental accessories."

Avoidance of orthogonal forms of space.
Multiplicity of geometric floor patterns.
Fusion of disparate architectural elements.

Creation of a human scale and production of perceptible (artistic) urban spaces.

Limitation of horizontal and vertical dimensions. Dimensions within the range of a person's vision to create perceptible and defined spaces.

DESIGN ELEMENTS

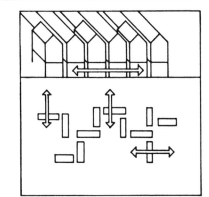

Town-planning level
Object level

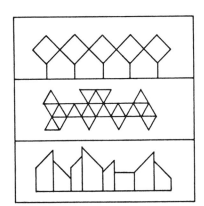
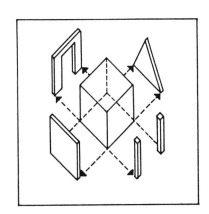

Town-planning level
Object level
Zone level

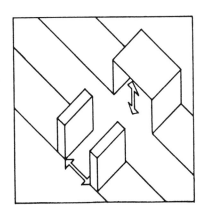

Town-planning level
Object level

A—RATIONAL PRINCIPLES

Expression of the structure; unity of materials and form; clear expression of the building process—that is, show how the space was created.

ARCHITECTURAL CHARACTERISTICS

Clear presentation of the principles of form and structure in accordance with the materials used.

Provision of a neutral space to allow demarcation for the differing uses or for emphasis on the interior finishes.

Simple, clear, and undivided subdivisions of space (neutral form of the entire space). Demarcation of the introverted functions from the extroverted spatial zones through a neutral demarcation of space.

Separation of the neutral structure of the space and the finishing elements of the space. Emphasis on these measures through the superimposition or interruption of the principles of the primary order.

Superimposition (interruption) of different geometric structures.

DESIGN ELEMENTS

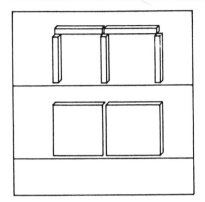

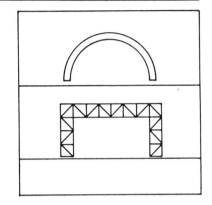

Object level
Zone level

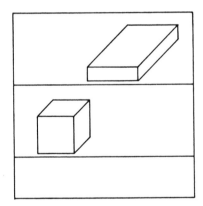

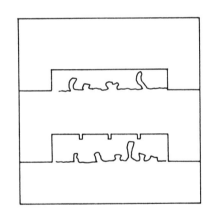

Object level
Zone level

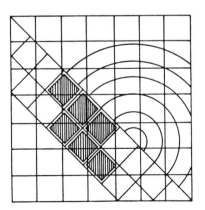

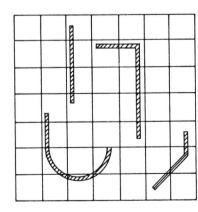

Object level
Zone level

A—RATIONAL PRINCIPLES

ARCHITECTURAL CHARACTERISTICS

Architecture as the sum of clear and geometric elements with similar emphasis on ''the artificiality of architectural spaces.''

Employment of unequivocal, clear, and familiar geometric surfaces and spatial volumes:

- circle/sphere
- square/cube
- rectangle/parallelepiped
- triangle/pyramid, etc.

Description of and/or emphasis on different zones for function and use. Separation into ''serving'' and ''served'' spaces.

Partitioning or clear separation of the different parts of a space in the overall design of the body of the building. Differentiation of individual user zones.

Creation of direct connections between spaces. Generation of a continuous sequence of spaces without ''intermediate spaces.'' Connection between the interior and the exterior space.

Lineup of individual and differentiated volumes of space without connecting and space zones, such as corridors or vertical connecting elements.

DESIGN ELEMENTS		PLANNING LEVELS AND GENERAL PRINCIPLES

Object level

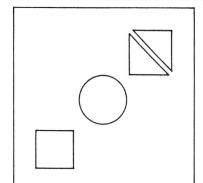 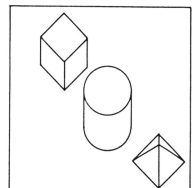

Object level

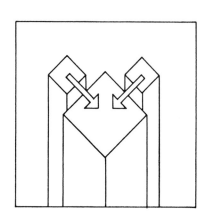 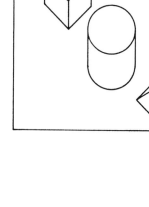

Zone level

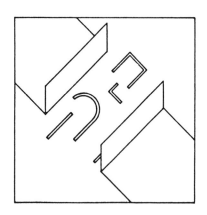 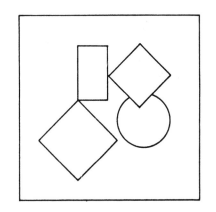

A—RATIONAL PRINCIPLES

Characterization of and/or emphasis on technical and functional conditions.

ARCHITECTURAL CHARACTERISTICS

Differentiation and emphasis on individual functional units or structural principles for the articulation of the body of the building.

Production of contradictions between the visual appearance of the architectural spaces and the added architectural elements. Demonstration of "complexity" through the introduction of disparate elements.

Superimposition of different principles of form/Rejection of symmetry/ Distortion of the original scales.

Clarity and readability of structural principles and fabrication of materials. Use of the least number of materials and construction methods.

Employment of a small number of appropriate and well-known materials and structures: brickwork/timber/ steel/concrete.

DESIGN ELEMENTS

Private living space

Public space

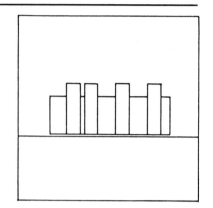

Object level
Zone level

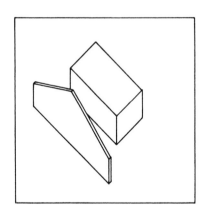

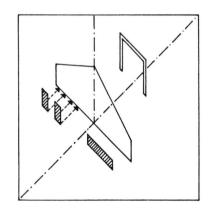

Town-planning level
Object level
Zone level

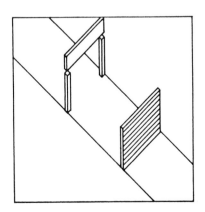

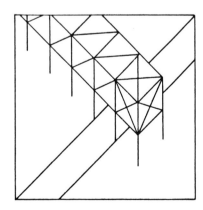

Object level
Zone level

B—SYMBOLIC PRINCIPLES

ARCHITECTURAL CHARACTERISTICS

Creation of different sequences of spaces to remind one of "places" as one walks through the spaces.

Combination of equal or similar plan units in differing arrangements. Alternation of narrow spaces (streets and paths) with wide spaces (squares).

Mixing of different functions to promote social contacts, in contrast to the separation of functions by the Modern Movement in the 1920s and 1930s.

Arrangement of different uses within the range of a building and direct connection of these zones—for example, along a network of public paths.

Architecture as a medium of communication. Reception of architecture through many layers. Architecture as a carrier of symbolism and information.

Supplementation of functional, structural, and other demands for a particular use by iconographic, metaphoric, and associated elements.

DESIGN ELEMENTS

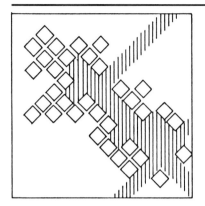
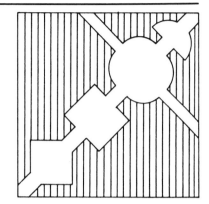

Town-planning level
Object level

Town-planning level
Object level

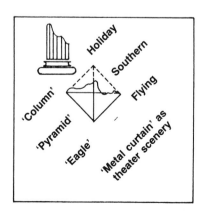
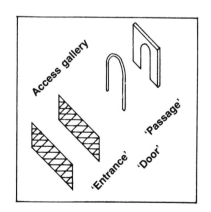

Town-planning level
Zone level

B—SYMBOLIC PRINCIPLES

ARCHITECTURAL CHARACTERISTICS

Emphasis on the "artificiality" of architecture. Separation of natural landscape and artificially created volumes of space. Separation of natural outdoor space from the artificial "interior space."

Limitation to clear and familiar geometric design elements emphasize the synthetic qualities of architecture in a natural landscape.

Design of the shape of a space in accordance with its "essential" quality—for example, designing spaces according to the shadows thrown by buildings and orienting them in accordance with the direction of the wind.

Allocation and orientation of the elements of a space in accordance with the desired social and physical conditions.

Differentiation and determination of the identity of a space through (natural) lighting.

Unequivocal allocation of light and dark zones or spatial elements in plan and elevation.

DESIGN ELEMENTS

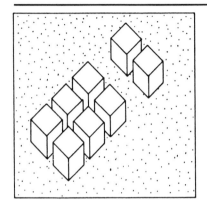

Town-planning level
Zone level

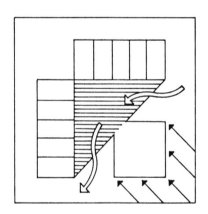

Zone level

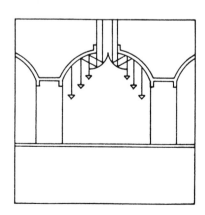

Zone level

B—SYMBOLIC PRINCIPLES

ARCHITECTURAL CHARACTERISTICS

Direct transition from one volume of the space to the next.
Integration of interior and exterior spaces.

Creation of "flowing" zones of space and "free" (from columns and wall slabs) arrangement of the elements that bound the space.

Separation of the façade and the body of the building (space). Façade as a "two-dimensional" source of information, independent from spatial group.

The space zones and floor areas are independent of their own formal needs and of the attached "principal façade."

Connection of spaces or buildings through a "chain of events," as a reminder of "places," and identification of specific spatial characteristics.

Sequence of distinctive artifacts to define space.
Sequence of distinctive forms of space or space boundaries.

DESIGN ELEMENTS

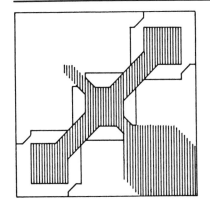

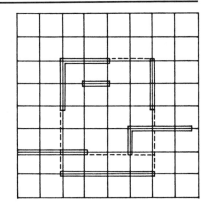

Object level
Zone level

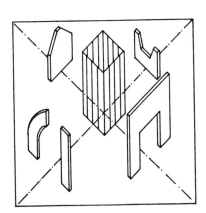

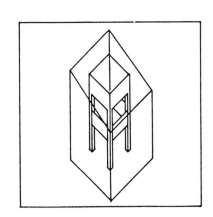

Town-planning level
Object level

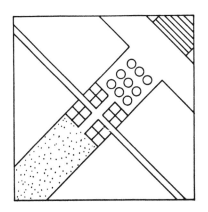

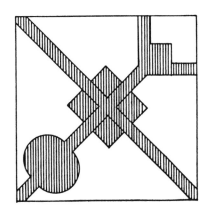

Town-planning level

C—PSYCHOLOGICAL PRINCIPLES

ARCHITECTURAL CHARACTERISTICS

Possibility of user participation in a personal design of the environment and stimulation of the fantasies of the users to encourage them to design their own space.

Creation of "primary" structures that can be appropriately "filled in" by the user. Provision of an "unfinished architecture," with separation of fabric/interior finishes and potential for self-expression by the user.

Creation of spaces so arranged as to stimulate the user's fantasy.

Offer of unfamiliar spatial forms to create new and unexpected spatial experiences.

Inclusion of the public space of the street within the building to obviate the psychological barriers between the public domain and the building and to promote social contacts.

Carrying paths "through" the building. No separation between exterior space and interior space.

DESIGN ELEMENTS

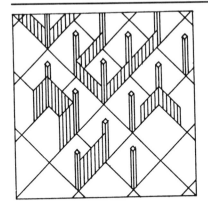

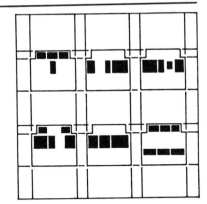

Object level
Zone level

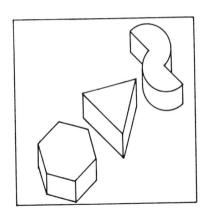

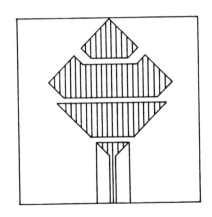

Zone level

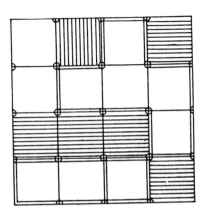

Town-planning level
Object level

Comparison/Contrast of Principles and Characteristics   **165**

Principles, Characteristics, and Planning Levels

The comparative juxtaposition of principles and characteristics shows that the individual "design elements" are of importance at different planning levels. Different design elements must be considered and used, even within a single design step. Some principles influence the architectural form, or the spatial coordination of the individual user zones of a building, exclusively at one level—for example, the town-planning level. The demands, and the space-forming effects that follow from them—for example, the connections of spaces and buildings through a chain of events that remind one of "places" or the identification of specific spatial characteristics—can largely be allocated to the town-planning level. In the design process, these aspects are particularly important for the formulation of goals in a town-planning situation, and the appropriate architectural characteristics are the formation of squares and streets, different elements of street furniture, and so on. The design of the details that result from this principle and their effect on the design of the spaces lie within the zone level at a later stage. On the other hand, there are principles whose effects extend over several levels, and the design process must be carried out with different characteristics at several levels. For example, the realization of the principle for the creation of "a great formal richness" needs to be considered at several levels with appropriate characteristics.

This principle should be considered at the town-planning level, for example, through the employment of geometrically varying building elements; at the object level, through the avoidance of orthogonal space forms; or at the zone level, through the addition of separate architectural elements for function, use, and structure. Design principles of this type can be followed through several planning levels in several steps, in an almost logical chain of reciprocal interdependence. In this process it has been shown that one can follow the principles in accordance with scientific and theoretical considerations in a logical chain or sequence through several levels, analogous to the structure of a tree; however, this applies only to a very small number of principles. Although an unequivocal limitation of individual planning levels and their specific design principles is not possible, the overwhelming number of principles are centered in one or at most in two levels of special significance.

For the actual design process, the dependence or choice of suitable architectural characteristics relative to a desired design principle is of great importance. The analysis has shown that the type of principle (that is, rational, symbolic, or psychological) has no particular influence on the frequency of or allocation to individual planning levels. Of decisive importance in bringing a particular principle to realization are the different constructional methods at the disposal of the architect.

The presentation of design elements following from the formulation of psychological principles is limited to elements that can be illustrated with sketches and comprehended in the design process. To avoid misunderstandings, it should be emphasized that the majority of psychological principles are not determined by individual design elements but through a series of relations and connections between different elements.

Principles and Architectural Trends

Social, political, sociological, and technical factors influence specific movements and trends in any particular architectural epoch. Thus, in the middle of the nineteenth century the revolutionary technology of steel production created a new architectural movement, from which new and previously unknown structural principles developed. In the 1920s new directions in architecture resulted from the contemporary debate on the problems of people living together in housing estates and high-rise apartment buildings, and by the rejection of the vocabulary of Eclecticism. Some of these new contributions lost their significance in the years that followed or were shown to be headed in the wrong direction, but some of the new ideas and movements, such as Functionalism and the so-called International Style, dominated the international development of architecture for many decades. All these new and different movements and trends were influenced by a multitude of factors, which were frequently contradictory.

The comparative tabulation of principles and characteristics has shown that the characteristics of individual architectural examples, on which the planning or design principles depend, can be classified into three types: rational, symbolic, and psychological. As mentioned above, any discussion of new trends in architecture is strongly influenced by a multitude of factors, and one can rarely present a single or dominant design objective. However, if one follows individual phases and lines of development to their origin or their starting point, then it becomes possible—by a conscious paring of marginal aspects—to allocate them essentially to three categories, which have rational, symbolic, or psychological goals. For example, the development of steel and reinforced-concrete construction in the nineteenth century was ultimately determined by the rational considerations of beginning industrialization. Similar aspects—that is, rational characteristics—determined the development of the early steel structures and tall buildings of the first Chicago School. The functional concept of architecture is also ultimately based on purely rational and frequently logical deductions from the comprehension of individual concepts of form, and consequently of design and of space. If one considers the central arguments of other architectural movements, it also seems possible to reduce them to a single, (usually their original), aspect. Through this paring it can be shown that the different movements and trends in architectural discussion from approximately the middle of the nineteenth century can also, by reference to the formulated principles, be classified essentially into three characteristics, rational, symbolic, and psychological (see diagram on page 169). This diagram shows the characteristic movements and their representatives arranged in chronological sequence and allocated to the appropriate principle.

This is an attempt to indicate the time at which any particular movement received special attention, and thus significance. An attempt has also been made to give the year of important and characteristic buildings (or an increase in the volume of buildings designed in accordance with the characteristic forms of the style). The change and sequence of the different movements and their goals, the beginning, and, for the time being, the end (at least the end of actual debate), of new styles of building is indicated by appropriate curves.

It is shown that individual movements generally come in waves. Until the middle of this century, rational and symbolic principles changed at almost regular intervals. Not until 1940 was there a more penetrating discussion of the psychological effects of architectural form on human perception and consciousness. At that point in time there was simultaneously a reduction in the length of the discussion of individual trends and statements and a decline in their significance. Until approximately the 1950s, the individual phases changed with an almost regular rhythm, and somewhat surprisingly, the

individual phases lasted for approximately the same period of time. Only since that time has there been a quick and at the same time short sequence of different contributions to the debate, which until today has run almost exactly parallel to the problems of contemporary architecture.

The comparative juxtaposition of individual periods in recent architecture and their dependence on different design principles show both the changes that have occurred and the interdependence of the various statements. The overwhelming number of designs can be assigned to characteristic epochs if one makes allowance for the original period of their design principles; they mirror the image and the architectural design form of a particular point in time.

Characteristics and Principles of Contemporary Architecture

The analysis of design principles and the comparison between architectural characteristics and their realization in buildings, using some examples from the most recent past, do not permit a valid or comprehensive conclusion as to the way architecture is likely to develop in the future. The problems of contemporary architecture, and their solutions in a few realized projects, are too topical to draw conclusions or

predict consequences for the future. However, by selection and limitation to a few typical architects who followed different goals, one can show variations that occurred during the last decade. The articulation of principles of different kinds mirrors a previously almost unknown multiplicity and plurality of different and even contrary concepts for the realization of architecture. The almost classical goals of the "rational" and "symbolic" principles have been substantially enlarged by a broad spectrum of "psychological" principles. The effect of architecture and of architectural forms on the human consciousness has become more noticeable. Users are offered the potential, through appropriate design programs and design concepts, for participation in the design of their environment. A closer integration of user and architecture is attempted through a changed world of architectural forms. Provision is made for a stronger identification of users with their architectural environment, within the available building technology.

In spite of different and often contradictory attempts to determine possible future developments, it can be shown that the majority of the efforts are clearly directed against the implications and consequences of the (often misunderstood) "inhospitable," sterile, and monotonous Modern

Movement. Special importance therefore attaches to the human perception of the effect of architecture, making due allowance for history. Familiar signs and symbols, which go beyond pure function and construction, contribute, according to Jencks, to making architecture an experience worthy of mankind, in the sense of a "double coding." An appeal is to be made to people and their sensibilities through appropriate design of social living spaces— that is, the design of the environment and the visual perception will go beyond a pure satisfaction of the functional demands. Contemporary architecture shows an unprecedented plurality of solutions. Differentiation between "right" and "wrong" is not possible, or at least it should be avoided. The analysis of the principles and their characteristics shows a multitude of possibilities that deserve to be taken seriously: how to produce, with the available elements of architecture, an environment that can be understood by people and is at the same time "humane." Of central importance is the clarification of the relationship between the principles and the architectural characteristics. For the design process it is of decisive importance to employ appropriate characteristics and to recognize possible consequences—that is, the potentials and the impediments posed by a particular principle.

PRINCIPLES AND ARCHITECTURAL TRENDS

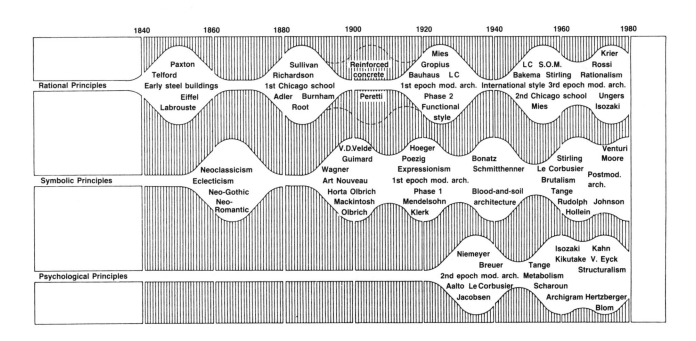

Summary

Using actual examples from contemporary architecture, a number of design principles supplied by the architects themselves, as well as their realization through architectural characteristics, have been analyzed. Central to this discussion was the analysis, with the aid of actual design problems, of the different movements and trends of recent years; this was done with particular reference to the preparation of a teaching aid for design. This led to a limitation to selected and characteristic examples, from which an intelligible and achievable presentation, from a teacher's point of view, of the design principles and their realization, appeared to be practicable. The direct juxtaposition of principles and their realization with architectural means—apart from the fact that it produces a design aid—can contribute to the avoidance of accepting, without sufficient consideration, superficial and formal aspects of design. Inadequate basic information about the interrelationship between the declared intentions of a design and the design concepts or projects developed therefrom have, in my opinion, frequently contributed to misunderstandings about the goals, for example, of the Modern Movement.

The graphic presentation of the characteristics in the form of sketches is intended both as an aid to design and as an introduction to architectural design. The formulation of goals is useful only if the architect has the characteristics for their realization at his disposal. The design as a model of a future reality consists of the sum of characteristics that illustrate the spatial and functional situation in terms of graphic symbols; that is, all the characteristics that are to be realized are in the first instance illustrated by means of two-dimensional constructions (sketches or drawings) or three-dimensional architectural models. Analogous to the design activity of the architect, the visual presentation is in the form of schematic sketches—the real elements of design. The analysis of the principles has shown that the overall form of a project is largely determined by relatively few design goals. A manageable number of basic and characteristic principles determine the overall concept of the design of space, and this is accomplished at different planning levels. By far the largest part of the remaining design decisions are apparently made afterwards, without the formulation of special goals. For a large part of the design decisions, in the case of the analyzed examples, the architects did not consider the formulation of detailed design principles to be essential.

The analysis has further shown that the formulation of design goals as unequivocal and logical chains in the sense of a hierarchical tree structure does not exist. Essential principles can be formulated for individual aspects of a problem, but only in a few exceptional cases can these be followed through as a hierarchical sequence from the town-planning level via the object level to the zone level. For this reason, the analysis of the individual principles has been presented without further subdivision. Venturi takes the formulation of principles so far that it seems to him legitimate to lay down the ultimate goals only after the completion of the design. To avoid misunderstandings, it should once more be emphasized that the goal of the analysis is purely the presentation of the design principles that the various architects themselves formulated. One's own interpretations through the analysis of interrelationships of space, structure, and form presume another procedure, and they are an important supplement within the framework of a general discussion of the theory of architecture and the history of art.

Architectural design consists of a graphic synthesis of a multitude of "individual decisions" (in the form of drawings). The decisive design factors can be made visible through a regressive and analytical dissection of the design into its original abstract and schematic parts. A knowledge of the graphic interrelationships between the principles and the characteristics at one's disposal can be of assistance in the development of new designs—that is, in synthesis. This does not, however, imply any statement on the significance of individual principles and their effect within the framework of the design of the environment through the medium of architecture. From these statements follow several possible steps in the discussion of the basis of architectural design.

An attempt has been made in the analysis to present the essential and characteristic principles that form the basis of planning. In this process no statements have been made about the relevance or possible consequences of these principles. Further investigation is needed, for example, to discover whether the principles of the removal of limitations or obstacles between the user or the public space and the building are sensible, or whether this creates additional user problems. The demand to create an architecture with the potential for reminding one of individual "places" is subjective and can at present not be considered a design principle with universal validity. Furthermore, each design proposition is influenced by specific factors and is thus transferable only under certain conditions.

An attempt has also been made in the analysis to contrast the design principles in each case with the built reality in the form of characteristics that illustrate the architectural form. This direct relationship is to be understood for each individual case as a subjective description of the connections between the required principles and the corresponding characteristics chosen. Whether the desired principles or goals have in fact been achieved through the architectural characteristics used would have to be the subject of a further investigation. Only through a careful examination of the performance of the reality in relation to the life of the user can a statement be made as to the success or failure of the desired design goals; indeed, one can only indicate the framework within which the user may recognize or perceive these defined intentions.

The principles presented in the analysis are the subjective thinking of individual architects, and they result mostly from experience, from restrictions inherent to the plan, and also from the simple wish to improve the design of the environment. One cannot, therefore, equate these principles with the possible wishes and needs of a later user.

By restricting the choice of the buildings examined to the most recent past, it was impossible within this framework to make any pronouncements about the results produced by the individual design goals after a certain period of use. Consequently, a further investigation might well analyze the effect of planning after some use in order to evaluate the success or failure of the defined goals, which could then be used for future planning. The analysis of the principles and the presentation of architectural characteristics by way of sketches has attempted to establish the connections between the potential for architectural realization and what the architect imagined. Goals or principles can only be attained by architects when adequate information exists about the elements to be used and the methods for handling them. Thus, a critical examination of these principles with reference to the general development of architecture, as well as an architectural critique of the individual projects that form the subject of this investigation, could only be undertaken with certain qualifications. The presentation and analysis of principles and their means for architectural realization yield information about the fundamental principles on which each particular design was based, and they may form an aide-mémoire and an instruction manual for the design activity of the architect. It should be possible to develop from these analyses individual steps for teaching the subject of design, both as teaching aids and as exercises, by examining projects that have been realized in practice both textually and in drawings. Knowledge of the origins or declared intentions that form the basis of a particular architectural design should help reduce a lack of understanding, empty formalism, and ill-considered plagiarism.

Notes:

Chapter 1

1. Georg Klaus, *Wörterbuch der Kybernetik* [Dictionary of cybernetics]. Vols. 1 and 2. Frankfurt am Main, 1969, p. 634.

2. Gerhart Laage, Holger Michaelis, and Heiner Renk, *Planungstheorie für Architekten* [Planning theory for architects]. Stuttgart, 1976, p. 35.

3. Harry Raudsepp, *Tätigkeitsbild des Architekten* [A picture of the activity of the architect]. Unpublished thesis. Faculty of Architecture, University of Stuttgart, 1972.

H. Sträb and W. Tonne, *Berufsfeldanalyse des Architekten* [Analysis of the professional activity of the architect]. Unpublished thesis. Faculty of Architecture, University of Stuttgart, 1972.

4. Horst Rittel, *Zur Methodologie des Planens im Bauwesen* [On the methodology of planning in architecture]. Essen, 1967.

John Luckman, "Zur Organisation des Entwerfens" [On the organization of design]. *Arbeitsberichte zur Planungsmethodik.* Vol. 4 (1970), p. 33 *et seq.*

H. Höfler et al., "Der Entwurfsprozess und Verfahren zum Methodischen Entwerfen" [The design process and procedure for methodical design]. *Arbeitsberichte zur Planungsmethodik.* Vol. 4 (1970), p. 79.

5. Heinrich Klotz and John W. Cook, *Architektur im Widerspruch* [Contradictions in architecture]. Zurich, 1974, p. 268.

6. Charles Jencks, *The Language of Post-Modern Architecture.* London, 1978.

7. Klotz and Cook, *Architektur im Widerspruch.* p. 47.

8. H. Klotz, *Architektur in der Bundesrepublik* [Architecture in the German Federal Republic]. Frankfurt am Main, 1977, p. 169.

9. Laage, Michaelis, and Renk, *Planungstheorie für Architekten.* p. 36.

10. Klotz, *Architektur in der Bundesrepublik.* p. 170.

11. J. Joedicke et al., "Entwerfen mit Hilfe Empirischer Gestaltkritieren" [Design with the aid of empirical criteria of form]. *Bauen und Wohnen,* No. 11 (Zurich, 1974).

12. HOAI (Honorarordnung für Architekten und Ingenieure). Fassung, 1976.

13. Robert Venturi, *Complexity and Contradiction in Architecture.* New York, 1966.

14. Robert Venturi, Denise Scott-Brown, and Steven Izenour, *Learning from Las Vegas.* Cambridge, MA, 1972.

15. H. Klotz, *Gestaltung einer neuen Umwelt* [The creation of a new environment]. Luzern, 1978, p. 8.

16. Klotz, *Gestaltung einer neuen Umwelt.* p. 8.

17. Jencks, *The Language of Post-Modern Architecture*.

Chapter 2

Development of the Analyses

1. Fritz Schumacher, *Der Geist der Baukunst* [The spirit of architecture]. Stuttgart/Berlin, 1938. Quoted by Gerhart Laage, Holger Michaelis, and Heiner Renk, *Planungstheorie für Architekten* [Planning theory for architects]. Stuttgart, 1976, p. 42.

2. Schumacher, *Der Geist der Baukunst*. p. 42.

3. Jürgen Joedicke, *Angewandte Entwurfsmethodik für Architekten* [Applied design theory for architects]. Stuttgart, 1976, p. 23.

4. Joedicke, *Angewandte Entwurfsmethodik für Architekten*. p. 23.

Piet Blom

1. Piet Blom, "Anmerkungen zur Kasbah" [Notes on the Casbah]. *Bauwelt* 37 (1974), p. 129.

2. Piet Blom and Johan Phaff, "Neues aus Holland und die seltsamen Ansichten des Piet Blom" [New ideas from Holland, and the curious views of Piet Blom]. *Bauwelt* 37 (1974), p. 1,218.

3. Piet Blom, "Anmerkungen zu Helmond" [Notes on Helmond]. *Bauwelt* 37 (1974), p. 1,225.

4. Piet Blom, "Die 'Kasbah' in Hengelo" [The "Casbah" in Hengelo]. *Bauwelt* 37 (1974), p. 645.

5. Piet Blom, "Mensagebäude der Technischen Hochschule Twente in Drienerlo" [The student refectory of the Institute of Technology Twente in Drienerlo]. *Bauwelt* 4 (1975), p. 96.

6. Piet Blom, "Helmond—Wohnwald mit Gemeinschaftszentrum" [Helmond—"wohnwald" with community center]. *Bauen und Wohnen* 1 (1976), p. 26.

7. Piet Blom, Auszüge aus einem Brief von Piet Blom an die Stadtverordneten und den Bürgermeister von Helmond [Extracts from a letter by Piet Blom to the councillors and the mayor of Helmond]. *Bauwelt* 8 (1976), p. 228.

8. Piet Blom, "188 Habitations Helmond." *L'architecture d'aujourd'hui* 196 (April 1978), p. 42.

9. Nathalie van den Eerenbeemt, "Het Speelhuis in Helmond—Gratwanderung zwischen Imitation und Interpretation [Het Speelhuis in Helmond—balancing on a knife edge between imitation and interpretation]. *Bauwelt* 29 (1978), p. 1,094.

10. Jürgen Joedicke, "Die holländischen Strukturalisten" [The Dutch Structuralists]. *Architektur im Umbruch*, 1980.

11. Paul Kessler, "Zwischen Kontrawänden und Dachwänden." *Bauwelt* 8 (1976), p. 225.

12. Arnulf Lüchinger, "Strukturalismus—eine neue Strömung in der Architektur [Structuralism—a new movement in architecture]. *Bauen und Wohnen* 1 (1976).

13. Paulhans Peters, "Die letzten zwanzig Jahre in der Architektur" [The last twenty years in architecture]. *Baumeister* 12 (1978), p. 1,146.

14. Peter Rumpf, "Holland in Wohn-Not?" [Holland short of housing?]. *Bauwelt* 20/21 (1975), p. 597.

15. Anonymous, "Architektonischer Kopfstand" [To stand architecture on its head]. *Deutsche Bauzeitung* 4 (1976), p. 14.

16. Anonymous, " 't Speelhuis—Helmond—Broschüre der Stadtverwaltung von Helmond" ['t Speelhuis—Helmond—pamphlet published by the town council of Helmond]. n.d.

Herman Hertzberger

1. P.D. Bosschart, *Centraal Beheer—De Bouwkosten und Bewaking*. Information pamphlet, n.d.

2. Herman Hertzberger, "Veränderung als Dauerzustand" [Alteration as a permanent state of affairs]. *Bauwelt* 30 (1971), p. 1,217.

3. Herman Hertzberger, Unveröffentlichte Planungserläuterungen zum Centraal Beheer [Unpublished commentary on the planning of Centraal Beheer]. October 1972.

4. Herman Hertzberger, "Verwaltungsgebäude der Centraal Beheer in Apeldoorn" [Office building Centraal Beheer in Apeldoorn]. *Bauwelt* 3 (1973), p. 130.

5. Herman Hertzberger, "Bürogebäude 'Centraal Beheer' in Apeldoorn" [Office building Centraal Beheer in Apeldoorn]. *Baumeister* 11 (1973), p. 1,407.

6. Arnulf Lüchinger, "Struktural-ismus/Architektur als Symbol den Demokratisierung, Ideen und Bauten von Herman Hertzberger" [Structuralism/architecture as a symbol of democratization, ideas and buildings of Herman Hertzberger]. *Bauen und Wohnen* 5 (1974), p. 5.

7. Herman Hertzberger, "Das Gebäude als Instrument für die Bewohner" [The building as an instrument for its inhabitants]. *Bauen und Wohnen* 5 (1974), p. 209.

8. Herman Hertzberger, "Struktural-ismus—Ideologie" [Structuralism—ideology]. *Bauen und Wohnen* 1 (1976), p. 21.

9. Herman Hertzberger, Beitrag im Katalog zur Biennale Venedig B 76 [Contribution to the catalog for the Biennale Venice B 76]. 1976.

10. Herman Hertzberger, "Amsterdam—Sloterwaart, Altersheim 'De Drie Hoven.'" *Bauen und Wohnen* 1 (1976), p. 12.

11. Herman Hertzberger, "Die Diagoon—Wohnungen in Delft—eine Form mit Vorschlägen" [The Diagoon apartments in Delft—a form with proposals]. *Bauwelt* 15 (1976), p. 474.

12. Herman Hertzberger, "Altenheim in Amsterdam" [Retirement homes in Amsterdam]. *Baumeister* 2 (1976), p. 132.

13. Herman Hertzberger, "Old People's Centre 'De Drie Hoven' at Amsterdam." *Architecture and Urbanism* 75:3 (1977), p. 67.

14. Herman Hertzberger, "Old People in Amsterdam." *Domus* 569 (April 1977), p. 10.

15. Herman Hertzberger, "Das Musikzentrum Vredenburg in Utrecht" [The music center Vredenburg in Utrecht]. *Baumeister* 4 (1980), p. 335.

16. Herman Hertzberger, "Architektur für Menschen" [Architecture for people]. In *In Oppostion zur Moderne* [In opposition to the modern movement]. Braunschweig, 1980, p. 142.

17. Jürgen Joedicke, "Die holläandischen Strukturalisten" [The Dutch structuralists]. In *Die Architektur im Umbruch* [Architecture in revolution]. Braunschweig, 1980.

18. Arnulf Lüchinger, "Struktural-ismus—eine neue Strömung in der Architektur" [Structuralism—a new movement in architecture]. *Bauen und Wohnen* 1 (1976), p. 5.

19. Arnulf Lüchinger, Struktural-ismus, unveröffentlichtes Buchmanuskript [Structuralism—unpublished manuscript for book]. 1978.

20. Michael Ritter, "Die fliegenden Holländer" [The flying Dutchman]. *Architektur Wettwerbe* 83 (September 1975).

21. Anonymous, Centraal Beheer, Informatie over het Gebouw van Centraal Beheer [Information pamphlet on Centraal Beheer]. n.d.

Hans Hollein

1. Friedrich Achleitner, et al., Ausstellungskatalog "Österreichische Architektur 1945–75" [Exhibition catalog—"Austrian architecture 1945–75"]. Vienna, 1976.

2. Kenneth Frampton, "Richard L. Feigen and Co. Gallery." *Architectural Design* 3 (1970), p. 129.

3. Dick Higgins and Wolf Vostell, *Poparchitektur—Concept Art.* (Dusseldorf, 1967).

4. Hans Hollein, "Städte—Brennpunkte des Lebens" [Cities—centers of life]. *Der Aufbau* (1963), p. 15.

5. Hans Hollein, Unveröffentlichte Entwurfserläuterungen zum Geschäftslokal Schullin, Wien [Unpublished commentary on the design of the Schullin shop, Vienna]. 1975.

6. Hans Hollein, "Fragments zur Architektur" [Fragments on architecture]. *Protokolle* 66 (1966), p. 105.

7. Hans Hollein, "Alles ist Architektur" [Everything is architecture]. *Bau/Schrift* 1/2 (1968), p. 1.

8. Hans Hollein, "Eine Industrie als Gastgeber" [An industry as host]. *Baumeister* 12 (1973), p. 1557.

9. Hollein, Unpublished commentary on Schullin shop, Vienna. 1975.

10. Hans Hollein, Städtisches Museum [municipal museum], Abeteiberg, Mönchemgladbach." *Baumeister* 5 (1975), p. 393.

11. Hans Hollein, "Museum in der Villa Strozzi, Florence." *Baumeister* 5 (1975), p. 414.

12. Josef Paul Kleihues, ed., "Hans Hollein." In Katalog zur Dortmunder Architekturausstellung 1976 [Catalog of the architecture exhibition, Dortmund, 1976].

13. Hollein, "Alles ist Architektur."

14. Hans Hollein, Unveröffentlichte Entwurfserläuterungen zum Städtischen Museum, Abteiberg, Mönchengladbach [Unpublished commentary on the design of the municipal museum, Abteiberg, Mönchengladbach]. Vienna, 1977.

15. Hans Hollein, Unveröffentlichte Entwurfserläuterungen zum Rathaus Perchtoldsdorf [Unpublished commentary on the design of the town hall, Perchtoldsdorf]. Vienna, 1977.

16. Hans Hollein, Unveröffentlichte Entwurfserläuterungen zum Österreichischen Verkehrsbüro [Unpublished commentary on the design of the Austrian Tourist Bureau, Vienna]. Vienna, 1978.

17. Hans Hollein, unpublished lecture at the Werkbund meeting in Darmstadt, 1978, on "Architecture as Language."

18. Hans Hollein, "Arte—Tekta 1978." *Bauwelt* 43 (1978), p. 1590.

19. Hans Hollein, Unveröffentlichte Entwurfserläuterungen zur Filiale Österreichisches Verkehrsbüro, Vösendorf [Unpublished commentary on the design of the Vösendorf branch of the Austrian Tourist Bureau]. Vienna, 1978.

20. Hans Hollein, "Österreichisches Verkehrsburo, Wien" [Austrian Tourist Bureau, Vienna]. *Deutsche Bauzeitung* 3 (1979), p. 26.

21. Hans Hollein, Architektur ist kultisch, rituell, ein Medium der Kommunikation [Architecture is worshipful, ritual, a means of communication]. Unpublished manuscript, 1979.

22. Hans Hollein, "ÖVB—Filiale Wien—Vösendorf" [ÖVB—Vienna branch—Vösendorf]. *Deutsche Bauzeitung* 3 (1979), p. 31.

23. Hans Hollein, "Platzgestaltung am Stephansdom" [Site form at Stephansdom]. *Deutsche Bauzeitung* 3 (1979).

24. Hans Hollein, "Umgestaltung Rathaus Perchtoldsdorf" [Renovation of the Perchtoldsdorf town hall]. *Deutsche Bauzeitung* 3 (1979), p. 34.

25. Hans Hollein, "MANtrans-FORMS," eine Ausstellung im 'National Museum of Design,' New York 1976–77" ["MANtrans-FORMS," an exhibition at the National Museum of Design, New York, 1976–77]. *Deutsche Bauzeitung* 3 (1979), p. 35.

26. Hans Hollein, "ÖSTERREICH-ISCHES Verkehrsbüro in Wien" [Austrian Tourist Bureau, Vienna]. *Baumeister* 2 (1979), p. 154.

27. Hans Hollein, Unveröffentliche Entwurfserläuterungen zum Sitz der Geschäftsleitung der Siemens AG [Unpublished manuscript on the design of the main offices of Siemens AG]. n.d.

28. Hans Hollein, "Erotische Architektur—wie könnte sie aussehen?" [Erotic architecture—how could it look?]. Source unknown.

29. Franz Mairinger, et al., Ausstellungskatalog "Sechs Architekten vom Schillerplatz" [Exhibition catalog "Six architects from the Schillerplatz"]. Academy of Fine Arts, Vienna, 1977.

30. Walter Pichler and Hans Hollein, "Absolute Architektur." In *Programme und Manifeste zur Architektur des 20 Jahrhunderts* [Programs and manifestos of the architecture of the 20th century]. Vol. 1. Bauwelt Fundamente, Berlin, 1964.

31. Karl Wimmenauer, "Media-Linien im Olympischen Dorf, München 1972" [Media lines in the Olympic village, Munich, 1972]. *Bauwelt* 16 (1975).

Arata Isozaki

1. Günter Bock, "Alles is Architektur—Ist Architektur Alles?" [Everything is architecture—is architecture everything?]. *Bauwelt* 43 (1978), p. 1,588.

2. Bill Chairkin, "Zen and the Art of Arata Isozaki." *Architectural Design* 47:1 (1977), p. 19.

3. Peter Cook, "Notes on Arata Isozaki." *Architecture and Urbanism* 1 (1972), p. 83.

4. Peter Cook, "On Arata Isozaki." *Architectural Design* 47:1 (1977), p. 30.

5. Philip Drew, "Arata Isozaki." In *The Third Generation*. London, 1972.

6. Arata Isozaki, "Review of Work." *Architecture and Urbanism* 1 (1972).

7. Arata Isozaki, "About My Method." *Japan Architect* 188 (August 1972), p. 22.

8. Arata Isozaki, *Selected Projects, 1960–1975.* Tokyo, n.d.

9. Arata Isozaki, "Two Museums in Japan" *Domus* 555 (February 1976), p. 14.

10. Arata Isozaki, "Comments on the Design of the Museum in Takasaki, Gumma Prefecture." *Architectural Design* 47:1 (1977), p. 37.

11. Arata Isozaki, "La métaphore du cube" [The metaphor of the cube]. *Architecture* 402 (April 1977), p. 62.

12. Arata Isozaki, "Musée d'Art Moderne, Takasaki." *Architecture* 402 (April 1977), p. 59.

13. Arata Isozaki, Contribution to the 1978 Symposium of the Werkbund. Author's manuscript.

14. Charles Jencks, "Isozaki and Radical Eclecticism." *Architectural Design* 47:1 (1977), p. 42.

15. Jürgen Joedicke, "Die Manera des Arata Isozaki" [The Maniera of Arata Isozaki]. *Bauen und Wohnen* 3 (1975), p. 100.

16. Jürgen Joedicke, et al., "Aus einem Gespräch mit Arata Isozaki" [From a conversation with Arata Isozaki]. In "Tradition und Probleme der Gegenwartsarchitektur" [Traditions and problems of contemporary architecture]. Unpublished report of a study tour of the Institut für Grundlagen der modernen Architektur und Entwurfen, Universität Stuttgart, 1975.

17. Josef Paul Kleihues, ed., Katalog zur Dortmunder Architekturausstellung 1976 [Catalog of the architecture exhibition, Dortmund, 1976].

Dortmunder Architekturhefte 3 (1976).

18. Teijiro Muramatsu, "Humanity and Architecture—Dialog with Arata Isozaki." *Japan Architect* 202 (October 1973), p. 89.

19. Adolfo Natalini, "Architettura di Ready-Made/Kamioka Town Hall." *Domus* 606 (May 1980), p. 8.

20. Jochen Tenter, "Rathaus in Kamioka" [Kamioka town hall]. *Bauwelt* 27 (1979), p. 1,156.

Louis Kahn

1. Stanford Anderson, "Louis Kahn in the 1960s." *Architecture and Urbanism,* 1975.

2. Richard D. McBride, "A New Mode or an Old Manner?" *Architecture and Urbanism* 08 (1977), p. 77.

3. Conrad U. Brunner, "Eine Haltung gegenüber Menschen" [An attitude toward people]. *Werk/Oeuvre* 7 (1974), p. 807.

4. B.V. Doshi, "Louis I. Kahn in India," *Architecture and Urbanism,* 1975.

5. Romaldo Giurgola and Jaimini Metha, *Louis I. Kahn.* Zurich, 1975.

6. Gerd Hatje, ed., *Lexikon der modernen Architektur* [Encyclopedia of modern architecture]. Munich/Zurich, 1963.

7. Bernhard Hoesli, "Louis I. Kahn—Findling im Fluss bett der Moderne" [Louis I. Kahn—a foundling on the shore of the modern movement. *Werk/Oeuvre* 7 (1974), p. 794.

8. Uttam C. Jain, "Obituary of a Poetic Genius," *Architecture and Urbanism,* 1975.

9. Jürgen Joedicke, *Architektur im Umbruch* [Architecture in transition]. Stuttgart, 1980.

10. Louis I. Kahn, "There Shall be Order." In *Programme und Manifeste zur Architektur des 20 Jahrhundert* [Programs and manifestos of the architecture of the 20th century], Ulrich Conrads, ed. Berlin, 1964.

11. Louis I. Kahn, "I Love Beginnings." *Architecture and Urbanism,* 1975.

12. Heinrich Klotz and John W. Cook, *Architektur im Widerspruch—Bauen in den U.S.A. von Mies Van der Rohe bis Andy Warhol* [The architecture of contradiction—buildings in the U.S.A. from Mies Van der Rohe to Andy Warhol]. Zürich, 1974.

13. Paul R. Kramer, "Ein Gespräch mit Louis I. Kahn" [A conversation with Louis I. Kahn]. *Werk/Ouevre* 7 (1974), p. 800.

14. Udo Kultermann, "Louis I. Kahn und die junge Generation" [Louis I. Kahn and the younger generation]. In *Die Architektur im 20 Jahrhundert* [The architecture of the 20th century]. Cologne, 1977.

15. Maki Fumihiko, "Contemporary Classic: Kimbell Art Museum." *Architecture and Urbanism,* 1975.

16. Chr. Norberg-Schulz, "Richards Medical Research Building." In *Vom Sinn des Bauens* [The meaning of a building]. Stuttgart/Milan, 1979.

17. H. Ronner, S. Jhaveri, and

A. Vasella, *Louis I. Kahn—Complete Work 1935–74.* Zurich, 1977.

18. Uelo Roth, "Begegnungen mit Louis I. Kahn" [Encounter with Louis I. Kahn]. *Werk/Ouevre* 7 (1974), p. 806.

19. Jonas Salk, "The Meaning of Man in the World Order." Speech on the presentation of the Philadelphia Award to Louis I. Kahn, 1971. In *Werk/Oeuvre* 7 (1974), p. 806.

20. Vincent Scully, Jr., *Louis Kahn.* Ravensburg, 1964.

21. Vincent Scully, "Works of Louis. I. Kahn and His Method." *Architecture and Urbanism,* 1975.

22. Peter Smithson, "Thinking of Louis I. Kahn." *Architecture and Urbanism,* 1975.

23. Manfredo Tafuri and Francesco Dal Co, *Architektur der Gegenwart* [Contemporary architecture]. Stuttgart, 1977.

24. Wulff Winkelvoss, "Das Programm is gar nichts, es ist nur Hindernis" [The program is nothing, it is only a hindrance]. *Baumeister* 7 (1974), p. 779.

Charles Moore

1. Gerald Allen, "Benign Perversity." *Architecture and Urbanism* 5 (1978), p. 41.

2. Kent C. Bloomer and Charles W. Moore, *Body, Memory, and Architecture.* New Haven, 1977.

3. Leland S. Burns, "Distance in Space and Time in a House Design."

Architecture and Urbanism, 5 (1978), p. 53.

4. Martin Filler, "Traveller from an Antique Land." *Architecture and Urbanism* 5 (1978), p. 47.

5. David Gebhard, "Charles Moore and the West Coast." *Architecture and Urbanism* 5 (1978), p. 47.

6. Rosemarie Haag Bletter, "Rite of Passage and Place." *Architecture and Urbanism* 5 (1978), p. 60.

7. Kazuhiro Ishii, "Deliberate Regression from Modern Architecture: Eleven Points/The Contribution of Charles W. Moore." *Architecture and Urbanism* 5 (1978), p. 25.

8. Charles Jencks, *The Language of Post-Modern Architecture.* London, 1978.

9. Jürgen Joedicke, "Zwischen Manieriertheit und Innovation" [Between Mannerism and innovation]. In *Architektur im Umbruch* [Architecture in transition]. Stuttgart, 1980.

10. Heinrich Klotz and John W. Cook, *Architektur im Widerspruch— Bauen in den U.S.A. von Mies Van der Rohe bis Andy Warhol* [The architecture of contradiction—buildings in the U.S.A. from Mies Van der Rohe to Andy Warhol]. Zurich, 1974.

11. Donlyn Lyndon, "Immanence: The Indwelling Spirit." *Architecture and Urbanism* 5 (1978), p. 36.

12. Mann/Dingler/E. Schirmbeck/ W. Stubler/Venturi/Moore, Seminar at the Institut für Grundlagen der modernen Architektur und Entwerfen. Universität Stuttgart, 1976.

13. Charles Moore, "University Club Santa Barbara." *Baumeister* 10 (1970).

14. Charles Moore, "Kresge College, Santa Cruz, U.S.A.." *Baumeister* 9 (1975), p. 797.

15. Charles Moore, "Design of the Historic Street." IDZ Symposium Berlin, 1975.

16. Charles Moore, "A Personal Explanation." In *In Opposition zur Moderne* [In opposition to the modern movement], by G. Blomeyer and B. Tietze. *Architecture and Urbanism* 5 (1978), p. 7.

17. Charles Moore, "The Work of Charles Moore." *Architecture and Urbanism* 5 (1978).

18. Paulhans Peters, "Die letzten zwanzig Jahre in der Architektur" [The last twenty years in architecture]. *Baumeister* 12 (1978).

Aldo Rossi

1. Carlo Aymonino, "Die Herausbildung des Konzeptes der Gebäudetypologie" [The deveiopment of the classification concept for buildings]. *Arch+* 39 (1978), p. 41.

2. Robert Delevoy, et al., *Rational-Architectural-rationelle.* Brussels, 1978.

3. Herbert Huppert, Aldo Rossi. Unpublished seminar given at the Institut für Grundlagen der modernen Architecktur und Entwerfen, University of Stuttgart, 1979.

4. Jürgen Joedicke, "Rationalismum" [Rationalism], in *Architektur im*

Umbruch [Architecture in transition]. Stuttgart, 1980.

5. Paul Katzberger and Dietmar Steiner, ". . . Dieses ist lange her . . ." [This is a long time ago]. *Umbau* 1 (December 1979), p. 18.

6. J.P. Kleihues, ed., Katalog zur Dortmunder Architekturausstellung 1976 [Catalog of the architecture exhibition, Dortmund, 1976]. *Architekturhefte* 3 (1976).

7. Paulhans Peters, "Rationalistische Architektur—der Beitrag Italiens/ Die letzten zwanzig Jahre in Architektur" [Rationalist architecture—Italy's contribution/The last twenty years in architecture]. *Baumeister* 12 (1978).

8. Bruno Reichlin and Fabio Reinhart, "Zu einer Ausstellung der Projekte von Aldo Rossi and der ETH—Zürich" [Comments on an exhibition of projects by Aldo Rossi at the Zurich Gederal Technical University]. *Werk* 4 (1972), p. 182.

9. Heinz Ronner, ed., Aldo Rossi (exhibition catalog). Zurich, ETH, 1973.

10. Aldo Rossi, "The Architecture of the City: Sketches for a Fundamental Theory of the Original Buildings." *Bauwelt Fundamente,* vol. 41 (Dusseldorf, 1971).

11. Aldo Rossi, "Une education realiste," [A realistic education]. *L'Architecture D'aujourd'hui* 174 (1974), p. 38.

12. Aldo Rossi, "Realismus als Erziehung" [Realism as education]. *Archithese* 19 (1976), p. 27.

13. Aldo Rossi, "Entretien avec Aldo Rossi" [Interview with Aldo Rossi]. *L'architecture d'aujourd'hui* 190 (April 1977), p. 39.

14. Rossi, "Une education realiste." p. 39.

15. Aldo Rossi, "Analogien" [Analogies]. *Bauen und Wohnen* 6 (1977), p. 216.

16. Aldo Rossi, "Das Konzept des Typus" [The concept of type]. *Arch+* 39 (1978), p. 39.

17. Aldo Rossi, "Haus Schmidt und das Problem der Monotonie" [Schmidt house and the problem of monotony]. *Werk/Architese* 17/18 (1978), p. 10.

18. Aldo Rossi, exhibition catalog. Rome, 1979.

19. Aldo Rossi, Project for Venice. In exhibition catalog, "10 immagini per Venezia." Venice, 1980.

20. Piero Sartogo, et al., Roma interrotta (exhibition catalog). Rome, 1979.

21. David Stewart, "Rationalism: A Rationale." *Space Design* 162 (1978), p. 3.

22. Manfredo Tafuri and F. Dal Co, *Architektur der Gegenwart* [Contemporary architecture]. Stuttgart, 1977.

23. Manfredo Tafuri, "Das Konzept der typologischen" [The concept of typological criticism]. *Arch+* 39 (1978), p. 48.

24. Manfredo Tafuri, "The Critique of the Language of Architecture and the Language of Architectural Criticism." n.d., place of publication unknown.

25. Adolf Max Vogt, et al., *Architektur 1940–1980*. Frankfurt, 1980.

26. Anonymous, 28/78 Architettura/ Cinquanta anni di architettura italiana dal 1928 al 1978 (exhibition catalog). Milan, 1979.

Oswald Matthias Ungers

1. Reinhard Rieselmann and O.M. Ungers, "Zu einer neuen Architektur" [Towards a new architecture]. In *Programme und Manifeste zur Architektur des 20 Jahrhunderts* [Programs and manifestos of the architecture of the 20th century], by Ulrich Conrads. Berlin, 1964.

2. Josef Paul Kleihues, ed., Katalog zur Dortmunder Architekturausstellung [Catalog of the architecture exhibition, Dortmund]. 1976.

3. Heinrich Klotz, *Architektur in der Bundesrepublik* [Architecture in the Federal Republic]. Frankfurt, 1977.

4. Heinrich Klotz, "Auf dem einsamen Weg vom De Chirico-Platz zur Treppe ins Nichts; Gespräche mit O.M. Ungers über dessen Entwurf zum Wallraf-Richartz-Museum in Köln [On the solitary walk from De Chirico Square to the staircase into nothing; conversations with O.M. Ungers on his design of the Wallraf-Richartz Museum in Cologne]. *Bauwelt* 1 (1978), p. 26.

5. Heinrich Klotz, "Der Fall Oswald Matthias Ungers" [The case history of Oswald Matthias Ungers]. *Deutsche Bauzeitung* 10 (1979), p. 15.

6. Martina Schneider, ed., "Entwerfen in der historischen Strasse" [Design of the historic street]. In *Arbeiten des Internationalen-Design-*

Zentrums Berlin zur baulichen Integration Alt/Neu. Berlin, 1976.

7. O.M. Ungers, "Für eine lebendige Baulust" [For a living love of building]. *Bauwelt* 8 (1961).

8. O.M. Ungers, "Entwerfen mit Vorseellungsbildern, Metaphern und Analogien" [Design with images, metaphors, and analogies]. *Bauwelt* 47/48 (1977), p. 1,650.

9. O.M. Ungers, "Thesen zum Entwerfen als morphologischer Prozess" [Theses on design as a morphological process], in Fünf Architekten zeichnen für Berlin/Ergebnisse des internationalesen Design-Zentrums [Five architects draw for Berlin/results of the International Design Center]. Berlin, 1979.

10. O.M. Ungers, "Kommentar zu einer humanistischen Architektur in Deutschland" [Commentary on a humanistic architecture in Germany]. *Das Kunstwerk* (April/June 1979), p. 133.

11. O.M. Ungers, "Museumserweiterung Schloss Morsbroich" [Extensions to the museum in the Morsbroich castle]. *Deutsche Bauzeitung* 10 (1979), p. 19.

12. O.M. Ungers, "Severiusviertel Köln" [The Severius Quarter in Cologne]. *Bauzeitung* 10 (1979), p. 22.

13. O.M. Ungers, "Mertenshof in Köln-Widdersdorf" [The Mertens Court in Cologne-Wittersdorf]. *Deutsche Bauzeitung* 10 (1979), p. 26.

14. O.M. Ungers, "Wohnbebauung Schillerstrasse-Berlin-Charlottenburg" [The housing development in Schiller Street, Berlin-Charlottenberg]. *Deutsche Bauzeitung* 10 (1979), p. 28.

15. O.M. Ungers, "Wohn- und Geschäftshaus, Berlin-Spandau/Hotel Berlin/Fassadengestaltung Woolworth, Berlin-Wedding" [Residential and commercial building in Berlin-Spandau/Hotel Berlin/Design of the facade for the Woolworth store in Berlin-Wedding]. *Deutsche Bauzeitung* 10 (1979), p. 37.

Robert Venturi

1. Philip Drew, *The Third Generation.* London, 1972.

2. David Dunster, ed., *Architectural Monographs 1, Venturi and Rauch.* London, 1978.

3. D. Hoffman-Axthelm, "Lernen von Las Vegas—hier in diesem Land" [Learning from Las Vegas—here in this country]. *Bauwelt* 16 (1979), p. 637.

4. Eckehard Janofske, "Robert Venturi oder der Versuch einer lebensnahen Architektur" [Robert Venturi, or the attempt to produce architecture that is close to life]. *Bauwelt* 16 (1979), p. 634.

5. Charles Jencks, *Post-Modern Architecture.* London, 1978.

6. Jürgen Joedicke, "Das Alltägliche als Vorbild" [Everyday life as an example]. In *Architektur im Umbruch* [Architecture in transition]. Stuttgart, 1980.

7. Daniel Juillard, ed., "Venturi et Rauch." *L'architecture d'aujourd'hui* 197 (June 1978).

8. Josef Paul Kleihues, ed., exhibition catalog of the architecture exhibit, Dortmund, 1976.

9. Heinrich Klotz and John W. Cook, *Architektur im Widerspruch/Bauen in den U.S.A. von Mies Van der Rohe bis Andy Warhol* [The architecture of contradiction/buildings in the U.S.A. from Mies Van der Rohe to Andy Warhol]. Zurich, 1974.

10. Paul R. Kramer, "Wir lernen von Rom und Las Vegas" [We learn from Rome and Las Vegas]. *Werk/Oeuvre* 2 (1974), p. 202.

11. Robert Maxwell, *The Venturi Effect: Architectural Monographs 1, Venturi and Rauch.* London, 1978, p. 7.

12. Stanislaus von Moos, "Bemerkungen zur Theorie und zum Schaffen bon Robert Venturi and Denise Scott Brown" [Comments on the theory and the creative activity of Robert Venturi and Denise Scott Brown]. *Architese* 13 (1975), p. 6.

13. Stanislaus von Moos, "Lachen, um nicht zu weinen—Interview mit Robert Venturi und Denise Scott Brown" [To laugh, so as not to cry—an interview with Robert Venturi and Denise Scott Brown]. *Architese* 13 (1975), p. 5.

14. Stanislaus von Moos, "Architektur im Alltag Amerikas—Venturi und Rauch" [Architecture in everyday America—Venturi and Rauch] (exhibition catalog). Zurich, 1979.

15. Stanislaus von Moos, "Von den Mucken des 'Alltags'—A propos von Venturi und Rauch" [Grumbling about the "working day"—with reference to Venturi and Rauch]. In exhibition catalog, "Architecture of Everyday America." Zurich, 1979.

16. Stanislaus von Moos, "Zweierlei

Realismus" [Two kinds of realism]. *Werk/Architese* 7/8 (1977), p. 58, and *Deutsches Architektenblatt* 5 (1980), p. 673.

17. Stanislaus von Moos, "Uber Venturi und Rauch, die Konsumwelt und den doppelten Boden der Architektur" [On Venturi and Rauch, the world of consumerism, and the dual floor of architecture]. *Bauwelt* 20 (1980).

18. Toshio Nakamura, "The Recent Nine Works by Venturi and Rauch." *Architecture and Urbanism* 1 (1978).

19. Jean-Louis Sarbib, "Complexité et contradiction d'une architecture pluraliste." *L'architecture d'aujourd'hui* 197 (June 1978), p. 2.

20. Denise Scott Brown, "Signals of Life/Symbols in the American City." *Architese* 19 (1976).

21. Vincent Scully, "On the Work of Venturi and Rauch." *Werk/Architese* 7/8 (1977), p. 4.

22. Robert Stern, "Venturi and Rauch: Learning to Love Them." In *Architectural Monographs 1, Venturi and Rauch*. London, 1978, p. 93.

23. Robert Venturi, *Complexity and Contradiction in Architecture*. New York, 1966.

24. Robert Venturi, Denise Scott Brown, and Steven Izenour, *Learning from Las Vegas*. Cambridge, 1972.

25. Robert Venturi and John Rauch, "Werkübersicht" [Review of their work]. *Werk/Architese* 7/8 (1977).

26. Robert Venturi, "A Definition of Architecture as a Box with Applied Decoration, and a Further Defense of the Use of the Symbolism of Everyday Life in Architecture." From exhibition catalog, "Architecture of Everyday America." Zurich, 1979.

27. Robert Venturi and John Rauch, "From Rome to Las Vegas" (exhibition catalog). Rome, 1979.

28. M. Weinberg-Staber, "Lernen von Venturi" [Learning from Venturi] (exhibition catalog), Zurich, 1979.

Chapter 3

1. J. Joedicke, *Angewandte Entwurfsmethodik für Architekten* [Applied design theory for architects]. Stuttgart, 1976, p. 29.

2. Fritz Schumacher, *Der Geist der Baukunst* [The spirit of architecture] (Stuttgart and Berlin, 1938). Quoted in Gerhart Laage, Holger Michaelis, and Heiner Renk, *Planungstheorie für Architekten* [Planning theory for architects]. Stuttgart, 1976, p. 41.

3. Schumacher, *Der Geist der Baukunst*. p. 213.

4. Schumacher, *Der Geist der Baukunst*. p. 252.

182   Notes

Index